..es. Ctr.
University Student Union / 2nd Flr.
5154 State University Dr.
Los Angeles, CA 90032
(213) 343-5471

Asian Pacific American SRC
5154 State University Dr. L.A. 90032
300 Gam / Romance of the Western
Chamber, The, 1973

The Romance of
the Western Chamber

WRITING IN ASIA SERIES

General Editor: Leon Comber

The Romance of
the Western Chamber

Translated and Adapted

by T.C. LAI & S.E. GAMAREKIAN

 Heinemann Asia

Hong Kong   Singapore   Kuala Lumpur

Swindon Book Company Limited

HEINEMANN EDUCATIONAL BOOKS (ASIA) LTD
Yik Yin Building, 321-3 To Kwa Wan Road, Kowloon, Hong Kong
41 Jalan Pemimpin, Singapore 2057
No. 2 Jalan 20/16A, Paramount Garden,
Petaling Jaya, Selangor, Malaysia

Heinemann Educational Books Ltd., London

Associated companies, branches &
representatives throughout the world

and
SWINDON BOOK COMPANY LTD. LOCK ROAD, KOWLOON

Printed by Bright Sun Printing Co.

CONTENTS

"But it is that brief look she gave that bedevils me; that look alone begins to drive me insane with love. And now she is gone to where paradise must be, leaving the willows and me in the mist."

"Treacherous woman! Why should your daughter consider me her Elder Brother?"

"What happened to all your big talk about unquenchable passion and consuming love? The great storm cloud threatens with thunder and lightning but not a single drop of water falls to relieve the drought."

"Gently now, your head on my pillow where the love birds flutter in joy. Now the golden hairpins and your hair is free. You are even more beautiful than I had imagined in my sleepless torment."

"I have gone through a lonely hell and worked myself to death to win the title of 'Lady' for my love...and now I find that you have dug my grave."

FOREWORD

I was delighted to read this translation of the "Western Chamber". It has changed the garb by clothing the story in English but has retained the tone and atmosphere, the play structure and the poetic handling of the language of the original. As a result, the reader has the feeling one gets when reading this old play in Chinese, even though it is an adaptation more than a servile translation.

The play in its earlier versions was a "literary drama". Its scenes were often acted on the stage but were even more often read and enjoyed as a story because of its literary quality.

There is an important difference between the play and the original story. In the original version, the lover Chang was a "heel" who abandoned his sweetheart. In the play, he is made faithful to the end and the story has a happy ending. In the original story, Nightingale was a strong character, superb in the role of the forsaken woman. The severely-decorous and well-secluded daughter of a prime minister, she had fallen in love with the handsome young man and, gripped in the throes of young passion, had given him her all in their nightly rendezvous. After his success in the examinations at the Capital, she waited in vain for his return as he, caught up in the sumptuous life at the capital, married the daughter of a rich family.

In the despicable tradition of "kiss and tell", he told everyone about his past romance and then, to justify his actions, wrote a poem comparing her to "an evil spirit capable of ruining a dynasty". Accepting the situation in a matter-of-fact manner, Nightingale married another suitor, and when years later her former lover called on her, she refused to see him. Research into the original writer's personal life has revealed these facts. The plight of Nightingale has been that of many a young miss, Chinese and Western, whose lover's mind has been changed by his success.

Lin Yutang

INTRODUCTION

No other love story has delighted the Chinese people as much as this one over the last twelve centuries.

The heartbreaking loneliness of shy Little Nightingale and the agony of the love-smitten scholar who is kept a safe distance away by the barriers of Confucian propriety have been well understood by generations of young Chinese whose mothers, like Little Nightingale's, have been more concerned with a proper marriage arrangement than with the hunger of young love.

In every Chinese love story, the key person is the inveterate matchmaker and in this story we have the saucy, piquant, fifteen-year-old maid-companion to Little Nightingale who knows when to tease, when to persuade, when to cajole and when to defy, and how to tell a few innocent and not-so-innocent lies when necessary to bring the inept poet-scholar and the indecisive Nightingale together.

The Romance of the Western Chamber had its beginning in "The Story of Ying-Ying",* a short story written in classical style by the poet-scholar Yuan Chen (778-831 A.D.) during the Tang Dynasty. The story is believed to have been based on an actual love affair Yuan Chen had with a young maid, although it does not seem likely that she was the daughter of a former prime minister as was the Ying-Ying of his story. In Yuan Chen's tale, the two

---

* The Ying is a bird similar to the nightingale. In Chinese, the repetition of a name puts it in the diminutive form, so Ying-Ying becomes Little Nightingale.

do not see each other again after the poet-scholar goes to the Capital for the Imperial Examination; when he attempts to visit her some years later, after both he and she are married, Ying-Ying refuses to see him.

During the centuries that followed the appearance of Yuan Chen's tale, story-tellers gave the story of Ying-Ying the kind of happy ending they knew their audiences preferred and added obstacles along the way to stretch out the suspense and comedy of the plot.

At the turn of the 12th century, during the Chin Dynasty, the poet-scholar Tung Chieh-yuan put the expanded story into a magnificent poem of eight books and more than fifty thousand characters that has come to be considered the greatest narrative poem in the Chinese language, titling it *Hsi-hsiang Chi*, or *The Romance of the Western Chamber*.

Some hundred years after the publication of Tung's epic poem, another poet-scholar, Wang Shih-fu by name, came along and expanded the story still further into a series of five Northern-style plays that were unprecedented in length and unsurpassed in their wealth of lyrical poetry. This series has, to this day, been regarded as the supreme masterpiece of Chinese drama, despite the criticism of the quality of the fifth play, the origin and authenticity of which has long been in question.

Wang's cycle of five plays was subsequently condensed into operas and plays of five acts that could be performed in a single evening and it is from one of these that this translation has been made.

This is not a word-for-word translation. It was

written to be read, rather than performed, so we have condensed the long monologues with which the characters introduce themselves as they enter. We have also eliminated the repetitious matter that was written into the beginning of each part to remind the audience when they returned from the interval where the players had left off.

The story contains many euphemisms that would not be understood by the non-Chinese reader, so we have had to be more explicit at these points. For example, the characters "clouds" and "rain", when put together, indicate the ultimate intimacy, the origin of this expression and its meaning going back to an ancient classical poem. "Clouds and rain" have subsequently been used so often to mean sexual intercourse that every Chinese reader understands its meaning, even those who have never read the original poem. Where expressions of this kind have been used, we have substituted comparable English euphemisms leaving the meaning, as must be the case with all euphemisms, to the imagination of the reader.

The Chinese versions of this story also contain references to proverbs, maxims, legends and teachings that would be understood only by readers of Chinese literature. Where practical, as in the references to the "Blue Bridge" and the "Temple of The Fire God", we have used explanatory footnotes. Where it was not feasible or was of lesser importance, as in the references to the legends of the "Three-Legged Crow" and the "Arrow of Hou Yi", we have let it pass with only a brief mention.

Where there is a reference to the teachings of Mencius and the concept of "propriety", we hope the

3

reader will understand the meaning from the context or, even better, that his curiosity will lead him to read something of the philosophy of Confucius, Mencius and the other Chinese sages on his own.

The reader will find much here to give him some insight into Chinese culture, philosophy and tradition, from the relationship between children and their parents to the significance of the Imperial Examination and tiny feet. Although the Chinese way of life is changing rapidly under the impact of modern technology and communication, the vestigial remnants of the centuries still remain.

The language of this translation is the language of the original. If it sounds overly sentimental and melodramatic, it is because that is the way it is in the Chinese versions, to which we have tried to be faithful.

T.C. Lai • S.E. Gamarekian

All illustrations are from Ming Dynasty woodblock prints.

DRAMATIS PERSONAE

LITTLE NIGHTINGALE: The shy sensitive nineteen-year-old daughter of the late Prime Minister Chu, one of the great beauties of her day.

RED MAID: The saucy fifteen-year-old maid-companion of Little Nightingale.

MOTHER: Madame Chu, wife of the late Prime Minister.

HAPPY BOY: Adopted son of the Chu Family.

CHANG KUNG: A poor but gifted scholar on his way to the Capital for the Imperial Examinations.

SUPERIOR: The Superior of the Monastery of Pu Chiu.

FA CHUNG: A monk at the Monastery.

HUI MING: Another monk at the Monastery.

'FLYING TIGER' SUN: Commander of a force of soldiers and horsemen stationed in Hochung, where the Monastery is located.

'WHITE HORSE GENERAL' TU: Boyhood friend of Chang Kung whose army is stationed near Hochung.

CHENG HENG: Nephew of Madame Chu.

PART I

ACT I

Scene 1. On the road to the burial ground at Po Ling

MOTHER: There, children. You can see it through the mist — the Monastery of Pu Chiu, built in honour of the Goddess of Heaven. And there, husband ... the Western Chamber.

What a grand procession we make! A weary old woman, a daughter, a young boy and a maid seeking shelter until the road to Po Ling is clear again.

I am of no consequence; it is our Little Nightingale who has been caught in this web of misfortune. We must now wait until the period of mourning is over before wedding her to our nephew Cheng Heng.

Remember when last we came, husband, how grandly we were honoured at the sumptuous tables? Who is there now to serve us but ourselves?

It matters not. Rest comfortably in your coffin. Of what consequence is it if we arrive at the burial ground a few days later? This journey can end only in tears with the plaintive cry of the cuckoo.

Scene 2. In the courtyard of the Western Chamber

LITTLE NIGHTINGALE: Alas, I am a prisoner again — a

petal freed by the wind, only to be captured by the stream. Can I tell the water my sorrows? Who can I blame but the wind?

Scene 3. On the bank of the Yellow River nearby

CHANG (Approaching the Monastery on horseback with his lute-boy following on foot): Look there, boy — the Yellow River — the great Yellow River! Its floating bamboo bridges guard it like black dragons, spitting angry foam from the wind-tossed waves at the autumn clouds. Come nightfall and the moon will send a ribbon of stars shimmering from the ninth heaven to the Eastern Sea, separating the States of Tsin and Chin, protecting Yen and passing by Chi and Liang to nourish the flowers of Loyang and sweeten the acres of Liang Yuan. It drinks from a hundred streams to the north and south on its relentless march to the sea with not so much as a backward glance at the homecoming boats rippling against it like leaden arrows.

Would that I could sail back to the heavens instead of drifting about like a tumbleweed! Having bored my way through the ancient classics and worn out my ink-stone, I am still no closer to the Capital than I am to the sun. Ten years of study by the light of the snow and the firefly and I am still nothing but an ordinary engraver of seals and mender of old books.

Yet, what is there to do but try again? I must get

back to the Capital for another sitting of the
Imperial Examinations after I see my old friend
'The Honest One' who defends Tu Kuan nearby.
A wise man, he, to give up a literary career for a
military one. Look at him now, a General with
10,000 men under his command.
This looks like a fine inn, lad. Take my horse.
   Ho! Innkeeper!
INNKEEPER (coming out): I am the innkeeper, Sir.
CHANG: Give me a front room and then look after my
   horse. But tell me, first, what there is to do around
   here.
INNKEEPER: The only place of interest is the
   Monastery, its hall as high as the blue sky, its tower
   scraping the clouds. People come from miles
   around to see it.
CHANG (to lute-boy): See to my horse and bags. And
   see about some food while I take a stroll along this
   path through the flowers and trees.

Scene 4. The Monastery

MONK: Good day, Sir. Where do you come from?
CHANG: From west of Loyang. I have heard much of
   your beautiful Monastery and I have come to wor-
   ship Buddha and pay my respects to the Superior.
MONK: He's not in just now. I'm Fa Chung. Would
   you like some tea?
CHANG: I would rather see the Monastery.
MONK: I'll get the keys so you can see the Hall of
   Buddha, the belfry, the pagoda and the Hall of

Lesser Dieties. By that time, the Master should be back.

LITTLE NIGHTINGALE (entering with Red Maid): Let us visit the Hall of Buddha.

CHANG (Aside, seeing Nightingale across the low wall): Who is this who suddenly fills my eyes with stars and soars my soul to heaven?

Such beauty cannot be from this time and place. This can only be a reincarnation of some romantic goddess whose spirit has roamed abroad for centuries unable to find peace.

Beauties I have seen by the hundreds, but never a maiden as delightful as this, laughing shyly into her flowers like a spring breeze. Her face must be as beautiful in anger as it is in joy.

LITTLE NIGHTINGALE: The moss-covered steps, red with fallen flowers, show no signs of life here. How quiet it is!

CHANG (aside): Lips of cherry and teeth of white jade. And the sweet round voice of a nightingale. How beautiful! Her waist, soft and graceful, moves with a thousand sighs and whispers, a willow shimmering in the evening breeze. Each step arouses in me a tender passion.

RED MAID (to Little Nightingale): Sister, there is someone on the other side of the wall.

(Nightingale looks across the wall and, seeing Chang, hurries back into the Western Chamber, followed by Red Maid.)

CHANG: How is it that the Goddess of Mercy is here?

MONK: Don't talk nonsense. It is the daughter of the

late Prime Minister.

CHANG: The most beautiful girl in heaven and on earth.
Her tiny feet alone must be worth 2400 taels of
gold*.

MONK: How can you tell at this distance? She is on
the other side of the wall and you are on this side.
Besides, she wears a long gown. How do you know
her feet are small?

CHANG: Look among the blossoms on the path; the
soft earth gives the answer. If I did not see the look
in her eyes, her walk alone would show the secrets
of her heart.

But it is that brief look she gave me that bedevils
me; that look alone begins to drive me insane with
love. And now she is gone to where paradise must
be, leaving the willows and me in the mist.

Even the pear blossoms in her courtyard are
inaccessible; the gate is locked and this wall might
as well be as high as the sky. How hateful a heaven
that doesn't help! There is nothing to do but wait,
I suppose. But how long? My mind races like a wild
horse and my heart throbs like a bear confused.

MONK: Don't start any trouble. The girl is gone.

CHANG: Her fragrance and movement are still in the
air; there is the scent of orchid and musk, and the
echo of tinkling jade. I see her lotus face aglow in
the willow where the gossamer branches hang
beaded with petals of peach blossoms.

You say she is the daughter of the Prime

A tael is 1½ ounces.

将一座梵王宫
疑是武陵源
莺如

Scholar Chang first sets eyes on Little Nightingale.

大雄寶殿

Minister but I say she is the Goddess of Mercy from the moon of the Southern Sea.

How can I go to the Capital for the examination now?

Can I trouble you to ask the Superior if I can rent a room in the Monastery so I can study for the examination? The inns are too crowded and noisy. I'll pay, of course.

(Aside, looking in the direction in which he last saw Little Nightingale):

My hungry eyes are ready to leave my head but there is nothing to be seen; my mouth waters and there is nothing to swallow.

That bewitching smile would have melted a man of iron and moved a man of stone. How can someone like me defend himself? I am beginning to lose my senses.

The flowers and willows may look as beautiful as before and the day as clear and sunny, but nothing is as it was any longer. She has gone and this place has suddenly grown desolate.

PART I

ACT II

Scene 1. At the Monastery the next day

CHANG: What a night! Not a wink of sleep after seeing that girl. Were it not for the monk, I might have got a little further. If I can get a room in the Monastery, I can study and, at the same time, at least fill my eyes with her. Let me get even half a room near her chamber and I'll be content. Do that much for me, Fa Chung, and I will have no complaints, whatever happens.

There are ways of winning such a treasure of jade and perfume. When the chance comes, I'll use every ounce of skill and charm at my command.

I once thought a painted face and shaped eyebrows shameful and deceptive, but on this lovely creature they arouse an indescribable passion that leaves me dizzy.

Fa Chung!

FA CHUNG (entering): My Master is expecting you. Wait a moment please.

(He goes into the Monastery and the Superior comes out, walking toward Chang.)

CHANG (Aside, on seeing the Superior): How extraordinary the snow of his hair and the absence of years in his face! How dignified his bearing! He needs only a light around him to look like a Buddha.

SUPERIOR: Please come in. I am sorry I was not here

15

yesterday to greet you. I hope you will excuse me.

CHANG: I have heard so much about this Monastery, I stopped off hoping to see you. This is my good fortune.

SUPERIOR: Where do you come from, Sir, and what is your name? Why do you journey in these parts?

CHANG: My name is Chang Kung but I am called 'The Fortunate One'. I am from the region west of Loyang as were my forbears who have been officials in various parts of the Kingdom. My father, who was well-known as President of the Board of Rites, died of an illness recently.

SUPERIOR: He must have left you a great fortune.

CHANG: He was a just and upright man during his entire life and died with an empty purse.

SUPERIOR: I knew him to be a great man, sociable and amiable, careful never to offend.

CHANG: That was my father — the clear wind and bright moon, upright and honest.

SUPERIOR: I presume you are on your way to the Capital for the examination.

CHANG: I am a humble scholar with no pretensions. It is not an official position I yearn for but knowledge, so I have come here for your instruction. But I have nothing to offer in exchange that is of any value. Like a poor scholar who can give nothing beyond a gift from his brush, I come empty-handed except for this tael of silver which I offer to the Monastery with a humble heart.

SUPERIOR: Why do this? You are on a long journey.

CHANG: It is such a small thing, barely enough for a cup of tea. Since I have come here specially to see you, please don't refuse this small gift.

SUPERIOR: I cannot accept it.

CHANG: It is hardly enough for food or firewood. (He sees Fa Chung and, turning toward him with the tael of silver in his hand, speaks softly to keep the Superior from hearing): This tael of silver is not much of a gift but if you could say something to the girl on my behalf, I will not forget you, either in this world or the next.

SUPERIOR: If there is something you would like, please tell me.

CHANG: It is really nothing special, Sir. It is just that the people and noise at the inn make it impossible to study. If I could have a room in the Monastery where I could also listen to your teaching, I would pay you whatever you wish.

SUPERIOR: We have several rooms from which you can choose.

CHANG: I would not need to use the kitchen. Nor would I need to use the room where the monks pray. I don't mind where you put me although I would like to be near the Western Chamber.

SUPERIOR: You could share my room with me.

CHANG: Please. I would rather not trouble you.

RED MAID (enters and approaches the Superior, bowing): I bring you wishes for a long life, Sir. My mistress has told me to ask when it would be possible to arrange a prayer service for the Prime Minister.

CHANG (aside): What a charming girl this is! She comes

17

Scholar Chang sees Superior.

like the daughter of a noble family, without the slightest trace of coquetry, bowing deeply to the Superior, the words coming with soft propriety from her cherry mouth.

What a delightful picture she makes in her plain white mourning gown, her face with only a hint of powder and rouge! Look at the way her eyes steal a glance at me as they flit about.

She is not the kind of girl you would expect to find making the bed that her young mistress might share with me. I will ask them to free her of her indenture and pay for her freedom personally if need be.

SUPERIOR (to Red Maid): I can arrange a prayer service for the Minister on the 15th of the Second Moon. I had better go now to see if the Hall of Buddha is ready.

RED MAID: May I go with you?

SUPERIOR: Of course. (To Chang): Please take a seat. I will return at once.

CHANG: Would it be all right if I came along?

SUPERIOR: Why not? Let us all go.

CHANG: Please go ahead. I will follow.

SUPERIOR: Thank you.

CHANG (whispering to Superior): May I have a word with you?

SUPERIOR: Please. Carry on.

CHANG: Don't you find this lovely girl attractive?

SUPERIOR: What a thing to say! I am a person who has renounced the idea of marriage and family.

CHANG: If you are not interested, how is it you are

so well groomed and so handsomely clothed?

SUPERIOR: What are you saying? Fortunately the girl did not hear. How embarrassing for her if she had!

CHANG: Heaven awaits in these corridors and chambers.

SUPERIOR (becoming angry):   Young man, this is not the kind of thing one would hear from the scholars of old. Are you not offending the dignity of this place? I am an old man. How could I be guilty of what you suggest?

CHANG: I am sorry, Sir. If you have no aspirations, I will say no more. Please do not be upset. But you should not be surprised that these ideas have crossed my mind.

Why is it that you have no men or boys to serve the Prime Minister's family? Why must the old woman use her maid as a messenger?

SUPERIOR: The old mistress is very strict and allows no men around her family.

CHANG (Aside, behind the Superior's back):   What a clever trick! You are being quite evasive.

SUPERIOR (to Red Maid):   The Hall will be ready tomorrow, on the 15th. Tell your mistress and her daughter that they can come and burn their joss sticks then.

(Red Maid goes into the Hall of Buddha.)

CHANG (to the Superior):   Why joss sticks?

SUPERIOR: The young mistress is very filial. She wants to burn incense before she puts aside her mourning clothes.

CHANG: Our gratitude to our parents for their toil

and pain is shown in so many different ways. Here is a mere girl intending to show herself a worthy daughter by burning joss sticks. And here am I, a drifting duckweed unable to find the time to do so much as burn some paper money.

May I give you some silver so I can participate in this ceremony in memory of my parents? If Madame Chu knows, I am certain she will not object. I just want to fulfil my duty as a filial son.

SUPERIOR (to Fa Chung): Let the gentleman have a share in the ceremony.

CHANG (aside to Fa Chung): Will Miss Chu come tomorrow?

FA CHUNG: Why shouldn't she come?

CHANG (aside): If she does, my contribution will have served its full purpose. It will be heaven just to look at Little Nightingale, so gentle and tender. I am ready to give her all my affection, indeed all of me. A brief touch, even by chance, would calm this great storm within me.

SUPERIOR (to Chang): How about a cup of tea in my room?

CHANG: I think I had better change. Here comes Red Maid from the Hall. There is something I wish to ask her.

SUPERIOR (to Red Maid): Some tea?

RED MAID: Thank you, but I am afraid my old mistress has been waiting too long for me already.

CHANG (to Red Maid): Give my regards to your young mistress. You are the maid of Little Nightingale, are you not?

RED MAID: I am. Why do you ask?

CHANG: My name is Chang Kung, although I am known as 'The Fortunate One'. I am from the west of Loyang and am 23 years old, having been born on the 17th of the First Moon during the first hour. I am not yet married and I . . .

RED MAID: Who is asking you for all that?

CHANG: May I ask . . . does your young mistress go out often?

RED MAID (annoyed):   You are a scholar and gentleman, are you not? Do you not know the teachings of Mencius? Contact between a maid and a man is not proper. A gentleman does not put on his shoes in a field of melons or adjust his hat under a plum tree*. Do you not also know the old saying: 'Do not look at what is improper, do not hear what is improper, do not say anything that is improper, and do not make any move that is improper'?

My old mistress is very strict, especially about things between men and women. We have no male servants more than five feet tall and no one over the age of 12 or 13 is allowed to enter farther than the middle hall unless called for. My young mistress was severely scolded the other day for going out of her room alone.

'You are a young maid,' the old mistress said.

---

*This old Chinese saying implies that a gentleman does not do anything to arouse suspicion with his actions. A man puts on his shoes in a field of melons when he is ready to leave it (with some melons, perhaps).

崔鶯鶯遺照

Little Nightingale.

'if you go out of your room without warning and a stranger sees you alone, it would be very shameful.'

You should abide by the principles of the sages and not interfere in other people's affairs. I can forgive you but if my old mistress knew what you said, there would be trouble. From now on, you should not ask what you have no right to ask. Ask only what is proper.

(She leaves.)

CHANG (aside): My feeling toward this girl is going to get me into a great deal of trouble.

So . . . the old mistress is so strict that nobody goes into the middle hall, is that it? If you are so afraid of your mother, young lady, why did you glance back yesterday? It is that look that is responsible for my present state.

If I am unsuccessful in this pursuit of love, it is probably because I have, in my previous life, offered Buddha a broken joss stick*.

I thought, not long ago, that my true love still awaited me at the remotest end of heaven. And now I find her no farther away than the Western Chamber. My body may be in this corridor but my spirit is already in her bedroom.

How can I let her know how I feel without her mother finding out? The old mistress is apparently afraid that her daughter can easily be seduced. It is obvious she doesn't like to see butterflies in pairs.

*A broken joss stick is an omen of a disappointment in love.

25

But this little miss looks young and impulsive. If I can get close enough to make some romantic overtures and succeed, why should I fear the restrictive coils of the old woman? I am certain I can outwit her.

We two will make quite a match — she with her virtue, beauty, talent and elegance; and I with my kindness, courtesy, modesty and frugality.

I find it impossible to free my mind of her lovely powdered face and pencilled brows, her soft jade-like neck and tiny feet, those delicate hands inside the red sleeves, and the graceful figure inside the embroidered skirt. Overshadowing my path for only half a day, her beauty has filled me with ten thousand thoughts and desires.

Ah, I have forgotten to say goodbye to the Superior.

(To the Superior): I beg to ask about the room.

SUPERIOR: Beneath the pagoda, on the western side, is a small chamber, tidy and clean. It should be just about right for you. You can move in anytime.

CHANG: I'll get my things from the inn.

SUPERIOR: Why not have something to eat first?

CHANG: It won't take long. I'll be back by the time the food is ready.

SUPERIOR: Come as soon as you can.

CHANG (to himself): Actually it wouldn't be too bad at the inn; there would at least be plenty of company. The Monastery is going to be so dreary and its bed so cold. With the solitary lamp giving me only my own shadow for company, I should be able to study but the nights are going to be long and sleepless.

With Nightingale so close, the day is going to be filled with ten thousand sighs and moans, and the night with ten thousand turnings of the pillow and poundings of the bed. She is a shy delicate flower ready to blossom, as smooth as jade, with the scent of rare perfume. I saw her so briefly I no longer remember quite what she looks like; yet I sit here with my head in my hands and can think of nothing else.

"I sit here with my head in my hands and can think of nothing else."

代相逢記不盡嬌模
樣則索手扺著牙兒
慢上的想　凌雲

PART I

ACT III

Scene 1. In the garden of the Western Chamber. Red Maid returns to find Little Nightingale among the flowers.

LITTLE NIGHTINGALE: Did you find the Superior?
RED MAID: Everything is being arranged for the 15th. I have just told your mother.

But let me tell you something. (She laughs.) It is quite funny.

Do you remember that young scholar we saw yesterday? I saw him when I went to see the Superior. When I took my leave, he was waiting for me outside the door. When I came out, he bowed deeply and said: 'My name is Chang Kung and I am known as "The Fortunate One". I come from Loyang, am 23 years old and am not yet married.'

But who asked him?

And then he said: 'Aren't you the maid of Miss Little Nightingale? Does she come out often?'

I don't know what he was after, mistress, but I stopped him short. I never saw such a fool.
LITTLE NIGHTINGALE (laughing): Say nothing to my mother about this. Let's arrange a table in the garden so we can burn some joss sticks. (They go in.)
CHANG (Aside, enters the garden on the other side of the low wall): What a beautiful night this is — a clear sky, a

bright moon and a soft breeze. Everyone seems to be asleep although Little Nightingale is supposed to be offering joss sticks tonight.

I'll stroll about and watch the moon awhile. If I catch a glimpse of Little Nightingale, I can at least satisfy my eyes. When I have time I shall seek the conversation of the learned monk but my soul tonight prefers verses and that bright star within the Western Chamber.

(Sings):   The jade universe is so clear,
The milky way shines gently through;
The moon is so bright,
Flower shadows fill the garden.

It begins to grow chilly as my ears strain for the sound of gentle footsteps. If she comes, I shall gather her warmly in my arms.

(The door leading from the Western Chamber to its courtyard begins to open and the voice of Little Nightingale is heard):
Now take the table out into the garden.

CHANG (Aside, on the other side of the wall): I hear the sound of a door opening and begin to sense a delicate fragrance in the air. If I move over this way . . . ahhhh . . . she is even more beautiful than when I first saw her.

(Little Nightingale and Red Maid appear.)

LITTLE NIGHTINGALE: A little nearer the stone wall.

CHANG (aside): The angel emerges from her heavenly palace and I can see her a little now through the trees. How slender and graceful! Her lilting walk along the flowery path shows how tiny her feet must be. That face is taking possession of my soul.

LITTLE NIGHTINGALE: Bring the joss sticks.

"That face is taking possession of my soul."

CHANG (aside): She begins to pray.

LITTLE NIGHTINGALE: In burning this first stick of incense, I pray that my father may soon ascend to heaven. In burning this second stick, I pray that my dear mother may live for a hundred years. And in lighting this one . . . (She becomes silent.)

RED MAID: Why are you silent? Let me make a wish for you.

I pray that my young mistress will find a nice husband soon and take me with her.

LITTLE NIGHTINGALE: So many things in my heart trouble me, I know not what to do but bow deeply and wait.

(She goes to the railing and sighs.)

CHANG (Aside, whispers softly): What disturbs your heart to make you sigh so? The eastern wind is quiet, and the air motionless. A lovely fragrance fills the deep night; and beyond the lingering mist of incense, the moon hangs like a mirror in the sky.

Why does she follow her prayers with such deep sighs? Is there some feeling in her heart for me? I shall sing a verse and see how she reacts:

> The moon glows bright this dark full night,
> The leaves cast shadows quiet;
> How can my soul face heaven so
> And still know nothing of it?

LITTLE NIGHTINGALE: There are verses coming from beyond the wall.

RED MAID: It sounds like the fool who is twenty-three and still unmarried.

LITTLE NIGHTINGALE: What a delightful poem! I shall

compose one of my own.

RED MAID: You two may as well do one together.

LITTLE NIGHTINGALE:

> In my orchid chamber I have lonely grown,
> Another spring passes and still I'm alone;
> Is it possible now that some wandering poet
> Will understand the sigh of love's moment?

CHANG: Behind the beautiful face is intelligence and wit. Who would have suspected it? She has responded to my verse with a clarity and feeling that befits a nightingale. If she would rhyme verses with me the whole night through, we would find our hearts and minds in harmony.

I'll make myself seen and see what she does. (He starts to climb over the low wall and Little Nightingale sees him.) She seems to be smiling.

RED MAID: There is someone there. We'd better go in.

CHANG (softly):   I come in answer to your wish. (aside): The maid is not being very helpful.

RED MAID: If we do not go in, your mother is going to be angry.

(They exit.)

CHANG (aside): What is that sound . . . ? Only the birds flying off in surprise. There is nothing left now but to return to my room across the red petals and confused shadows.

(The bell tolls the midnight hour.)

CHANG (aside): What am I to do now, Little Nightingale, left alone with the bright moon, the cold dew and the shadows? What kind of fate is this that keeps us apart?

How can I find my way back through this deserted garden? The wind sways the bamboos and I am miserable.

How can I live if she does not care for me? But if she does not care for me, for whom does she care? Her eyes give her away. We did not speak but we understand each other's hearts.

How am I to sleep tonight?

Scene 2. Chang's room in the Monastery

CHANG (aside): Alone with my lamp, an inconstant blue, my bed is cold. The moon is gone and a bone-piercing wind rustles the paper strips that hang to keep the ghosts at bay. That solitary pillow and lonely coverlet would move a heart of stone to sadness.

But I have no regrets about this night except that I am too tired to sit up and sleep is not likely to come easily.

Some day, in the shade of a willow, when the mist closes in and the clouds obscure the moon, we will vow eternal love and find peace and joy in the start of a new life.

It all began today, with my verse and hers. My future is not in the Capital. It is under yon peach tree. It is there that I shall wait for it.

PART I

ACT IV

Scene 1. In the Monastery. The Superior appears, followed by Fa Chung.

SUPERIOR: Today is the day for the Memorial Service. Let the monks begin to beat the wooden fish*, the bells and the gongs. Since the old mistress and her daughter are not yet here, let Master Chang make his offerings first. If Madame Chu asks who he is, tell her he is a relative of mine.

CHANG (aside): Swirls of smoke from the smouldering joss sticks fill the room like a storm, conjuring up visions of sea dragons locked in combat. The paper strips of the worshippers hang in great profusion and the clear sounds of the bell echo from the rain-washed pines. With the service ready to begin, this lover's greedy eyes cannot wait to receive their own offering.

SUPERIOR: You light your joss sticks first. If the old mistress asks who you are, just say you are my relative.

CHANG (lighting joss sticks): To all those who are living, I wish longevity; to all those who are dead, happiness in heaven. I pray specially for my

*The wooden fish is a hollowed-out block of wood with a fish-like shape.

37

grandfather and father. And I pray, secretly, that Red Maid will not be mischievous, that the old mistress will not discover what is happening, and that the dogs of misfortune will not be ferocious. Please, Buddha, make it possible for us to meet as soon as possible.

(Mother enters with Little Nightingale.)

MOTHER: Superior, please light the joss sticks for me.

CHANG (aside): Buddha awards my sincerity — the angel has descended. I thought at first it was the jade fairy from the blue heavens but it is indeed my beloved coming to pray. How can this unhappy body and ailing spirit win and hold one whose beauty could easily bring down a kingdom?

> Behold, a cherry mouth so small,
> Her nose, the purest jade of all,
> Her face, a blossom for a pillow,
> Her waist, as supple as the willow,
> Her spirit's brightness fills the night,
> Her grace an elegant delight.

SUPERIOR: Madame Chu, a word if you please. I have a relative, a young scholar who no longer has his parents, who would like to take part in the ceremony so he can fulfil his duties as a son. On the spur of the moment, I granted him his wish and hope you do not mind.

MOTHER: Your relative is my relative, Sir. Let me greet him.

(Chang greets her. A commotion slowly develops as the young monks, seeing Little Nightingale, begin to joke, laugh and make faces.)

38

CHANG   (Aside, noticing this commotion):   The Superior
    has become so old he obviously cannot see what is
    happening. The monks are using each other's heads
    for drums, behaving as though this were a New
    Year celebration.
        The longing in my heart becomes unbearable,
    Little Nightingale. But what is this? Tears like
    drops of dew on a blossom. The whimper of a bird
    lost in the dark forest. For your father? Or me?
(There is a sudden gust of wind.)
SUPERIOR: The wind has blown out the oil lamp.
CHANG: Let me light it.
LITTLE NIGHTINGALE   (to Red Maid): He is so young,
    so gallant; and yet, underneath it all, he must be
    learned and wise.
        But he puts on such a show, day and night,
    fussing about in the garden, outside my window, in
    the corridor, in the Hall of Buddha, always sighing.
    When does he rest?
CHANG (to himself):   She is looking at me, and with
    such longing. I wonder what she is thinking?
        How annoying those gongs are! And the noisy
    chanting of the monks! They take the beauty from
    this first meeting.
(The Superior ends his prayers and signals the monks to
proceed with the burning of the symbolic paper money for use
in the next world.)
SUPERIOR (to Mother):   The ceremony is over. You
    and the young mistress may now return to your
    quarters.
CHANG (aside): Alas, she is leaving. I wish we could

The Memorial Service.

start all over again.

My joy always ends abruptly, always too soon. The bell sounds, the cock crows and the worshippers depart, leaving Buddha to himself once more.

PART II

ACT I

Scene 1. The camp of 'Flying Tiger' Sun and his regiment

'FLYING TIGER': The entire country is in chaos with the new emperor on the throne. Here am I, Sun Piao, the 'Flying Tiger', supposed to be guarding Hochung with five thousand foot soldiers and horsemen and, instead, am told to rob and ravage the people by my Commander-In-Chief, General Ting. Ah, well ... if he's getting what he can out of this, why shouldn't I?

That girl in the Monastery, Little Nightingale, the daughter of the Prime Minister—now there's a prize worth taking. They say she has a face as beautiful as the lotus in spring and the charm of the most famous beauties of old.

Why not, now that her father is dead? Why should I alone behave like a gentleman?

Officers! Soldiers! Listen to my command! Prepare to leave tonight for Hochung. And quietly! Let every man put a plum in his mouth and a muzzle on his horse.

(To himself): I shall kidnap Little Nightingale and make her my wife. To have a wife of great beauty has been my lifelong wish.

Scene 2.   At the Monastery

(Shouts and the sounds of gongs and drums announce the arrival of 'Flying Tiger', his flags and banners flying in the breeze.)

FA CHUNG: Master! Master! The army of 'Flying Tiger' is at our gates, shouting that they have come to kidnap Little Nightingale. What are we to do? How can they attack this Monastery?

MOTHER (very agitated): What are we to do, Superior? We must find Little Nightingale.

(They exit.)

Scene 3.   Little Nightingale's bedroom

LITTLE NIGHTINGALE (Aside, not yet aware of the arrival of 'Flying Tiger'): My mind wanders confused and I can scarcely breathe. I know not what to do and this sad melancholy drives itself deeper into my heart each time a falling blossom reminds me of the passing of spring.

> Words with passion written,
> Go deeper when the moon is full;
> Voiceless, the falling blossoms
> Cry out that the wind is cruel.

Each moment of sadness has taken its toll, and now, with the springtime near its end, my silk robe has become so loose. How many more nights of loneliness can I bear?

It would be better if I kept the curtain closed to the fragrant breeze and did not see the pear

44

blossoms scattering in the rain. If I stay away from the balcony, I will not be set dreaming by the passing clouds. How sad to see the wind take the petals from the trees and torment them without pity!

I dreamt about the beauty of spring last night and say goodbye to it this morning. If only it would stay!

How many beauties of this world have pined away like this for someone on the other side of a garden who was no nearer than the ends of heaven!

RED MAID: My young mistress looks pensive and sad. If I perfume her coverlet with the smoke of the sandalwood burner, she will have a pleasant sleep.

LITTLE NIGHTINGALE: It is no use. If you used the most fragrant orchid and musk, my coverlet would still be cold and lonely.

It was so obvious last night that his verse was intended to bring me to him, yet I am still no nearer than before. I am as restless during the day as I am at night. I am unable to take a leisurely stroll without wanting to sit, and unable to sit without wanting to move. My thoughts are filled throughout the day of love. And him.

It seems, Red Maid, that I cannot leave my room without you following me like a shadow.

RED MAID: It is not my idea. Your mother has ordered me to stay close to you.

LITTLE NIGHTINGALE: Why is my mother so worried that she has to tie me up so tightly? Is she afraid I shall do something unworthy?

RED MAID: You do not normally behave this way.

Since you saw that man you seem to be unnaturally quiet. Why is that?

LITTLE NIGHTINGALE: When I used to see a strange man, I would turn red and run away. But when I saw this man, I was immediately attracted. When he composed a verse for me, my reply came easily and naturally and showed my true feeling. My verse was in such harmony with his . . .

Who can arrange a meeting with my neighbour to the east? Who will be the shuttle?

SOLDIER (shouting): You in the Monastery! Listen! Send Little Nightingale out to marry my General and everything will be all right. Refuse and the Monastery will be burned to the ground and everyone butchered. Not one person will be spared.

MOTHER (rushing to Little Nightingale): Oh my poor child! 'Flying Tiger' is outside with five thousand brigands saying that he wants you as his wife. What are we to do?

LITTLE NIGHTINGALE: My soul is so frightened it is ready to leave its shell. Is there no way to escape, no place to hide? Now that my father is not here, who can help us? The clouds of dust and the thunder of the drums and gongs fill me with terror.

I feel like the beloved concubine of the T'ang Emperor whose beauty cost him his kingdom.

But why me? Perhaps they do not want me. Perhaps it is the monks they are after? This rascal is a traitor who robs and kills people. Is there no wise man here who can devise some means to destroy these brigands?

46

MOTHER: I am sixty and not too young to die. But my child is young and still unwed. What can be done?

LITTLE NIGHTINGALE: There is nothing left but to hand me over so your lives may be saved.

MOTHER: How can I let you marry this bandit? It would bring great shame to our family, whose history is without blemish. Among our ancestors there is no man who ever committed a crime and no woman who ever remarried. How can I bear to hand you over to this traitor?

SUPERIOR: Let us go to the hall underneath the corridor so we can discuss this with all the monks and see what can be done. (Exits.)

MOTHER: What are we going to do?

LITTLE NIGHTINGALE: You might as well hand me over. There are, after all, some advantages:

First, it would save you.

Second, it would save the Monastery from destruction.

Third, the monks would be spared.

Fourth, no harm will come to my father.

And fifth, little brother, 'Happy Boy', still so young, will be . . .

HAPPY BOY: It doesn't matter. Don't worry about me.

LITTLE NIGHTINGALE: You must continue the line of the Chu family. If I do not agree to the demands of the brigands, the monks will be hacked to pieces and the Monastery burned to the ground.

My kind mother will be lost from me, my father's body left unburied and, my little adopted brother ... what would happen to you? Then there will be no one left in the family.

The best thing is for me to hang myself with my white silk scarf. Then you can give my dead body to the traitor. Giving him half is better than giving him all. Don't worry about me.

But wait. I have an idea. Suppose I offer to marry the person who succeeds in driving off the bandits and restoring peace. Anyone would be better than 'Flying Tiger'.

MOTHER: This sounds like a better idea. The person may not be one who fits in with our social position but he would still be better than the traitor.

Superior, tell everyone here, be he a monk or an ordinary person, that whoever drives off the bandits will have Little Nightingale as his wife.

CHANG: I have a plan.

MOTHER: What is it?

CHANG (looking toward Little Nightingale): There is an old proverb: 'When there is a great prize, a brave person will come forward to claim it.'

LITTLE NIGHTINGALE (becoming excited): I hope he is the one who can do it.

MOTHER: As I have just told the Superior, the one who expels the brigands can marry my daughter.

CHANG: Please return to your chambers and let me take care of this matter.

MOTHER (to Little Nightingale and Red Maid): Take Happy Boy back to our quarters and wait there for me.

LITTLE NIGHTINGALE: At least one man shows a little concern. All these monks stand around without the slightest interest and only this young scholar, who has nothing to do with us, is anxious to help. I pray that he is not like other scholars who have only theories to offer.

I hope his plan works and that the jade is not destroyed with the stone. I hope that the brush-pen of my young scholar can sweep away the five thousand.

(Exits with Red Maid and Happy Boy.)

MOTHER: Now, what is your plan?

CHANG: I must have the help of the Superior.

SUPERIOR: Look, young man, I am no warrior. Please find someone else.

CHANG: Don't be afraid. I'm not asking you to fight. Just go out and tell 'Flying Tiger' that Madame Chu says that Little Nightingale cannot come now because she is still in mourning for her father. Tell him that if he wants to marry Little Nightingale, he must wait three days, until the religious ceremonies are completed and the mourning clothes put aside. Little Nightingale will then be sent out in her bridal clothes. In the meantime, he must withdraw his men from the Monastery the distance an arrow can fly.

Tell him that if he takes Little Nightingale while she is still in her mourning clothes, it will bring bad luck to his army.

SUPERIOR: What happens after three days?

CHANG: You will see.

PART II

ACT II

Scene 1. The Monastery

SUPERIOR (calls out): I have a message for the General.

'FLYING TIGER': You'd better send Little Nightingale out here and be quick about it.

SUPERIOR: Her mother has asked me to tell you that she agrees to give up Little Nightingale but that you must wait for another three days, until she can take off the clothes of mourning that she wears for her father. She also asks that you stop beating the drums and withdraw from the gate of the Monastery the distance an arrow can fly until then, when she will send Little Nightingale to you in bridal clothes. She asks me to remind you that it will be bad luck to take Little Nightingale while she still wears her mourning gown.

'FLYING TIGER': All right. I'll give you three days. If there is no Little Nightingale singing in my tent by then, I will kill every one of you.

Tell the old woman I will make a good son-in-law.

('Flying Tiger' and his men begin to withdraw.)

SUPERIOR: Now what? If nothing happens in three days, we will all be dead.

CHANG: I am only a humble scholar but Tu Chueh, known as the 'White Horse General', is an old friend of mine. At this very moment, he has a

50

hundred thousand men under his command at Tu
Kuan. If I send him this letter, I am certain he will
come to our rescue. But his headquarters are
forty-five miles from here. Who can deliver the
letter?

SUPERIOR: Excellent! If the 'White Horse General'
comes, our worries will be over.

We have an apprentice here called Hui Ming, a
lazy chap who likes only to eat and drink, but one
with spirit. If I ordered him to go, he would refuse,
but if I made it a kind of challenge he would do it.

SUPERIOR (loudly to the monks standing around): I have a
letter here to be delivered to General Tu at Tu
Kuan.Who wants to take it? Who here has the
courage to go through the lines of 'Flying Tiger'?
Who would dare try?

HUI MING: I would dare! I don't recite the Lotus
Sutra like these other monks. I've already forgotten Emperor Liang's 'Guides For Repentance'
and I've put aside my robe and cowl, but I am a
brave man. Besides, I love a good fight. Put an
iron-tipped stave in my hand and I will fight to the
death. I may not know how to enter the Hall of
Buddha for meditation but I know how to enter a
tiger's den for slaughter.

It is not a question of being greedy or bold but
the tasteless diet of vegetables and bread I get here
makes me hungry for stronger fare. These five
thousand men should satisfy my great appetite.
They need not be roasted, baked, fried or stewed;
I'll take them raw.

Keep your thin soups, noodles, pickled leaks and bean curd. I'll make dumplings of minced meat with these men. And the ones I don't consume now, I'll pickle in salt.

CHANG: Do you really dare?

HUI MING: Who are you to ask such a question? Ask me not if I dare but if my master wishes to use me. The name of 'Flying Tiger' may be feared throughout the south but he is an evil man, filled with greed and lust. How can he be tolerated?

CHANG: Why, after leaving your family to study the sacred books and mystical rituals, do you want to go out and fight?

HUI MING: I have grown bored with sacred books and impatient with meditation. But my knife has a new blade and my stave stays polished with use.

I am not much of a monk nor am I a man of the world, but I have no use for those who spend their lives in a monastery in reading and meditation and, at a time like this, care not if the Monastery is burned to the ground.

I may not be as religious as some of the others here but I am not ashamed of my courage and heart. If you want someone to take the letter on this perilous mission, I am the man.

CHANG: Will you go by yourself or do you want some help?

HUI MING: Let me have some young monks with banners and some novices with clubs and staves. You keep everything here under control and we will carry out our task boldly.

CHANG: Suppose they stop you?

HUI MING: Stop me? How can they? An angry glance from me is enough to turn a calm sea into a tempest. The sound of my voice will echo and re-echo off the mountains and cliffs into a mighty roar. Each step will create an earthquake, and when I raise my arm, the gates of heaven will shake.

Those afar will be laid low with one swipe of my stave; those nearby will be cut in two with my blade; those who are small will be kicked like a ball; and those who are large will have their skulls smashed.

CHANG: When can you start?

HUI MING: I am ready! Sound the drum to lend me strength and give me the blessing of Buddha. When I shout my battle-cry, unfurl the banners and watch the courage of the bandits ooze away. (He leaves.)

CHANG (to Mother and the Superior): Pray be at ease. The letter will bring the 'White Horse General' flying.

Scene 2.   In the camp of the 'White Horse General'

'WHITE HORSE GENERAL' (to some of his officers): I have been getting some disquieting reports from the area under General Ting's control, reports of corruption and bad treatment. But I do not know how accurate they are, so I do not feel I can take any action against him yet.

Never forget the basic principle of strategy set

down by Sun Tzu, one of the greatest military strategists of all:

'Although you have the authority from your sovereign, there are solutions you do not have to pursue, there are armies you do not have to attack, there are cities you do not have to besiege, and there are positions you do not have to contest. There are even orders from your sovereign that you do not have to follow.'

The reason I do not act against General Ting is not that I lack the authority but that I lack information. Let us see what our scouts have to say when they return today.

(Hui Ming enters with a soldier.)

HUI MING: I come from the Pu Chiu Monastery, which, at this very moment, is surrounded by five thousand brigands under 'Flying Tiger'. He threatens to destroy it unless they give him the daughter of Prime Minister Chu whose body is there for its final prayers. A visitor called Chang, 'The Fortunate One', has asked me to deliver this letter in the hope that you will send help.

'WHITE HORSE GENERAL' (takes letter and reads):

'Beloved Elder Brother,

'Two years have passed since I was last in your noble presence, two years in which you have always been in my thoughts. When I left home to go to the Capital, I intended to visit you as I passed this way but the journey so exhausted me I became ill.

'I am somewhat better, having taken a rest in

the Pu Chiu Monastery, but the place has suddenly come under attack.

'The widow of Prime Minister Chu, after bringing his coffin to the Monastery for the usual religious ceremony, has been set upon by an outrageous bandit-general who, with a force of five thousand men, is demanding that she give up her beautiful daughter to him.

'I am overwhelmed with fury but what can I do? When the Government learns of this, who will be to blame? If you send a battalion to save us, you would not only show your worth to your sovereign by saving many innocent lives but would show yourself a faithful brother. And the Prime Minister, who is now beyond the nine streams, will never forget your great deed.

'I pray for a favourable reply and am looking in your direction for the arrival of your great banner. I salute you.'

(To Hui Ming):   Go back. I will follow immediately.

HUI MING: You'd better come quickly.

'WHITE HORSE GENERAL': I do not have the authority to set out on this campaign but, as the great strategist Sun Tzu said, 'A general in the field does not always require orders from his sovereign.'

(To his officers): Get five thousand men and horses ready to move out immediately to save Chang Kung at the Monastery.

Scene 3. Two days later at the Monastery

MOTHER: Two days and still no reply.

CHANG: Hold on! There is some commotion outside. It must be 'Flying Tiger'. No! Wait a minute! They have been surrounded by the horsemen of the 'White Horse General'.

'WHITE HORSE GENERAL' (entering to and bowing Madame Chu): My apologies for not having done something before this about these bandits. I am at fault for all the shock and fright suffered by the Prime Minister's family. I hope you will forgive me.

CHANG (bowing to the General): Seeing you here, the clouds are pushed away and the sun shines once more.

MOTHER: My children and I would like to repay your kindness. Please let me know what we can do.

'WHITE HORSE GENERAL': This is my duty. Why talk of payment?

(To Chang): Why have you never come to see me?

CHANG: I did not make the trip because I have not been well. I would accompany you on your return but Madame Chu has promised to give her daughter to me in marriage. Can I trouble you again, this time to act as the go-between?

'WHITE HORSE GENERAL': This is wonderful! Of course! Congratulations!

MOTHER: Let some food and tea be prepared.

'WHITE HORSE GENERAL': Please do not bother. I must still round up some of the brigands who have not yet been captured.

('Flying Tiger' is brought in under guard.)

'WHITE HORSE GENERAL' (to 'Flying Tiger'): I was going to
    behead all of you and report to my sovereign on
    the manner in which General Ting has been
    carrying out his duties. But I suppose some of the
    captured are innocent, so we'll give them the
    benefit of the doubt and just give you a good
    flogging. After one hundred strokes, you can take
    your men back to camp.
('Flying Tiger' is led off.)
    Well, my scholarly brother, all that is left is for
    you to be married to the lovely Little Nightingale
    whose beauty has brought about the attack and
    the rescue.
MOTHER: I'm afraid my daughter is not good enough
    for this young hero.
CHANG: Why not stay for the wedding dinner?
'WHITE HORSE GENERAL':   I must return to camp. But
    we shall have a celebration the next time we meet.
(He leaves.)
MOTHER: You have done us a great service, Scholar
    Chang. You must come and stay with us. We have
    many rooms here; I will arrange one of them for
    you so you can move in tomorrow. Red Maid will
    come and fetch you when it is ready and then we
    can have a talk.
(She leaves.)
CHANG (to the Superior): It is now up to you. Nothing
    stands in the way of my marriage to Little
    Nightingale, does it?
SUPERIOR: It is only a matter of time.

PART II

ACT III

Scene 1. The Western Chamber, the following morning

MOTHER: Everything is ready for Scholar Chang. Red Maid, go quickly and tell him to come. And don't let him give you any excuses.

Scene 2. Chang's room in the Monastery

CHANG (Aside, alone in his room): What can be keeping Red Maid? I have washed so many times I have emptied two pitchers of water.

RED MAID (on her way to Chang's room): Five thousand brigands swept away like a cloud and our family saved from disaster! Who would have expected a letter to a general to become a marriage contract? This young man deserves the best we can give him.

CHANG (aside): Today I shall be feasted and honoured at the Eastern Pavilion, and bedded down in a quiet, richly-furnished room. No longer will my pillow and blanket be cold.

Footsteps! There seems to be someone coming this way.

RED MAID (Aside, seeing Chang through the window): How elegant he looks in the pure, white robe and golden belt of the graduate! I can see why he has touched the heart of Little Nightingale. As cold as I am, he even touches mine a little.

(She coughs outside his door.)

CHANG (aside): There is someone there.

RED MAID (aside): I can imagine him nervously getting ready to bow, his hands clasped. What should I say? Ten thousand wishes of prosperity and good fortune, master? That's good enough.

(She knocks.)

CHANG: Who is it?

RED MAID (aside): How quickly he answers!

CHANG (opening door and bowing): Come in.

RED MAID: My old mistress invites you for dinner. Please do not . . .

CHANG: I'm coming. I'm coming. Will Miss Little Nightingale be there?

RED MAID(aside):Before the word 'invite' comes out of my mouth, the word 'yes' has already come out of his. As soon as he sees Little Nightingale, it will be 'Miss, Miss, Miss' and 'yes, yes, yes'. Whenever a scholar hears the word 'invite' it is like a military command that his stomach makes him eager to obey.

CHANG: Who will be there?

RED MAID: No one. This dinner is only to help us all recover from the shock of the past few days and show our appreciation to you. No one else has been invited, not even the Superior, and no gifts will be accepted. This dinner is for you and Little Nightingale.

CHANG: I have no mirror. Would you look me over to

Scholar Chang accepts invitation to dinner.

see if I am presentable?

RED MAID (aside): This mad silly scholar has polished his brow so much its brilliance dazzles the eyes. He struts about looking so worried at his own shadow that the poor miserable wretch sets my nerves on edge.

CHANG: What will there be to eat?

RED MAID: Some old rice and pickled turnips.

CHANG (aside): How strange all this! A few days ago, when I first saw Little Nightingale, I hardly anticipated this turn of events. It must have been predestined.

RED MAID (aside): The meeting of a man and his true love happens neither by chance nor design. It is the will of heaven.

CHANG: When a man is successful at one thing, he is successful at a hundred things; when he fails at one thing, he fails at many. Does your mistress really love me?

RED MAID (aside): I have heard that men of genius are so sentimental that the slights of a woman they love can drive them to suicide.

(To Chang): You will have proof of the sincerity of my mistress tonight.

CHANG (aside): Things grow in unison throughout nature. The branches of trees intertwine and two stems grow on the legendary lotus.

RED MAID (aside): Heaven has endowed him with such lofty sentiments; I can understand now why he has fallen in love with Little Nightingale.

(To Chang): For the joy and happiness you seek tonight you must be gentle and kind. Little

Nightingale is young and innocent, and without experience. Be very gentle. When you see all her bewitching beauty in the light of the lamp and are joined in happy union, you will be unable to restrain your ardour.

CHANG: You go first. I will follow with my belongings.

RED MAID: The ground is red with flowers, adding gaiety to this happy hour. Hurry, Sir, my mistress waits. Behind the peacock screen of jade, the bridal bed has been prepared, a midnight moon and Mandarin birds of love across its gold-sprinkled curtain. As you two play your sweet melody, the phoenix flutes and wild swan lute will join in happy harmony.

CHANG: I am a poor scholar without money for wedding gifts. What am I to do?

RED MAID: Neither money nor gifts are needed. This marriage, pre-ordained by Heaven, can be celebrated without delay. Ride the male and female phoenix today and we will be able to see the meeting of the Weaving Maid and Cowherd* in the sky tonight.

You are very fortunate to be tied together without the use of even a thread of red silk**.

*Two legendary lovers, doomed to an eternity of loneliness as stars, who find their way into each other's arms only once a year, on the 7th day of the seventh moon, when the magpies form a bridge with their wings for them across the Celestial River (Milky Way).
**Red silk is used to tie up wedding gifts.

CHANG: Will there be no guests?

RED MAID: My mistress has only her family. And you, Sir, have no companions. Free from all fuss, it will be a quiet ceremony.

CHANG: You go ahead. I will be there as soon as I can.

RED MAID: I hope your modesty does not make it necessary for me to return for you. My mistress awaits. It is better to obey than to make a show of modest politeness, as the saying goes.

(She leaves.)

CHANG (aside): What will Madame Chu say to me when I arrive? Probably 'Come in, Master Chang. Have some wine with Little Nightingale before you become man and wife.'

Once we are wed, I will lead her into the bridal chamber, loosen her belt and take off her clothes. The male and female phoenix will then roll into one as we reach the stage where the storybooks usually say: 'If you wish to know what happened, read the next chapter.'

PART II

ACT IV

Scene 1. The Western Chamber. Red Maid arrives followed by Chang.

MOTHER: Welcome, Master Chang. And our heartfelt thanks. If it were not for you, we would not be here today. We owe our very lives to you. This dinner is in no way a return for what you have done for us but I hope you will not consider it entirely unworthy.

CHANG: The good fortune of one person often brings good fortune to many. The defeat of the bandits was due entirely to your being a person of good fortune. My part in it is not worthy of mention.

MOTHER: Bring the wine. Here, Sir, this cup for you. Please sit down.

CHANG: I cannot think of sitting in your presence.

MOTHER: Please. You know the old saying about it being better to obey than be polite. Red Maid, tell Little Nightingale to come in.

(Red Maid goes into Little Nightingale's room.)

LITTLE NIGHTINGALE (aside): The table is ready and the music about to begin. How soft this blend of incense and flowers that flows around me to the one who rescued me from ruin! Show him every attention and treat him with the utmost respect. It is only right and fitting.

RED MAID: You are ready early. How beautiful you

look, your skin a rare translucent porcelain so delicate and fragile one dares not breathe on it or touch it! How lucky is Master Chang!

LITTLE NIGHTINGALE: You are talking nonsense without rhyme or reason.

RED MAID: Heaven has created you to be the wife of a nobleman.

LITTLE NIGHTINGALE: Stop your jabbering, so noisy and loose. He is not that fortunate. And I am not that beautiful.

RED MAID: One thing is clear. The two of you, once so sad, are now very happy.

LITTLE NIGHTINGALE: If my longing for him and his longing for me are now joined in love, this is an occasion for a special feast. But my mother seems to have other ideas.

RED MAID: What do you mean?

LITTLE NIGHTINGALE: You don't know the way my mother's mind works. She is afraid she will have to give a dowry and has decided to save money by making the dinner for Master Chang also serve as a marriage celebration.

His help was worth all the money our family could give him for the rest of his life. And what are we giving him? Nothing. How much has the arrangement of this match cost her? Nothing. And yet she is afraid of spending too much.

(She begins to leave her room.)

MOTHER: Come in, daughter, and pay your respects to your Elder Brother.

CHANG (aside): Elder Brother? This does not sound

very good.

LITTLE NIGHTINGALE (aside): She has changed her mind!

RED MAID (aside): A death-blow has just been aimed at this marriage.

CHANG (aside): I am caught in a field of thorns, unable to move, as if dead. I am so confused I do not know what to say, so dejected I can neither sit nor stand.

Treacherous woman! Why should your daughter consider me her Elder Brother?

Suddenly the water is rising and I am caught underneath the Blue Bridge*. The Temple of The Fire God is consumed in flames** and the two fish that swim side by side in the pure blue sea are forced to part.

MOTHER: Red Maid, bring some hot wine for your Young Mistress and her Elder Brother.

LITTLE NIGHTINGALE (aside): My sorrow is too much to bear. The light has gone out in my heart and the sparkle from my eyes. I cannot lift my head to speak, but what is there for two lovers to say when their first meeting ends so dismally?

(She pours some wine into Chang's cup as tears begin to appear in her eyes.)

---

*In the poem "The Blue Bridge", a young man waiting to meet his love under the bridge refuses to leave until she comes. The water keeps rising and drowns him before she arrives.

**Another tragedy, in which a young man, waiting for his love in the Temple, falls asleep. When she arrives, she decides not to wake him and leaves but when he awakens, he thinks she did not come. He bursts into flame and burns the Temple down around him.

CHANG: I am not a drinker.

LITTLE NIGHTINGALE: Remove the wine-cup, Red Maid. How can he drink? How can the happiness of the Western Chamber have vanished like an empty dream?

He sits there downcast, without spirit, his shoulders and hands immovable, a man incurably ill. He wipes his eyes and his sleeve is wet, but he makes no sound. You have driven him to his death, Mother. Is this what you want?

MOTHER: Daughter, you must give your Elder Brother a cup of wine.

(Little Nightingale fills another cup for him.)

CHANG: I have already said I do not drink.

LITTLE NIGHTINGALE: Please. Please drink it. It may ease the pain in your heart.

MOTHER: Red Maid, take your mistress back to her room.

(Red Maid and Little Nightingale begin to leave, but Little Nightingale stops.)

LITTLE NIGHTINGALE (aside): Who can explain this sudden change of mind, this strange riddle? She tries to console him but only succeeds in making him more unhappy.

A beautiful woman is always unlucky in love. What am I to do?

A moment ago he was full of gladness, now he is filled with tears. If it were not for his letter, what would my mother have done; if it were not for me, why would he have written it?

If it is my beauty that has brought me to this

lonely crossing, I will no longer colour my face like a blossom or my lips like cherries.

This endless sorrow is as deep as the sea and as broad as the earth, as vast as the sky and as high as a mountain.

What is it you want, Mother? You hunger for his help as if he were the God of the Eastern Sea and then you are bitterly cruel. You flatter him with sugary words and then trick him into being an Elder Brother.

You have crushed the twin buds of this flowering, destroying a future that held such bright promise. Do the burdens of old age make it necessary to disappoint the hopes of youth?

How different it might have been if you did not do what you are doing now. How I would love you if you had been more honourable?
(She exits with Red Maid.)

CHANG: I am overcome with wine and beg to make my farewell. But before I go, let me say something if I may. When tragedy threatened, why did you say you would give Little Nightingale in marriage to her rescuer? I did not secure the aid of the 'White Horse General' because I wished to eat at your table. When Red Maid came to summon me this morning, I was looking forward to the joy of marrying beautiful Little Nightingale. Why have you suddenly flung at us the titles of Elder Brother and Younger Sister?

MOTHER: You have saved our lives and I am grateful, more than you know. But Little Nightingale has already been promised to someone else — long ago, when her father was still alive. He is not with us because he is at the Capital for the Examination.

What are we going to do when he returns? What I wish to do is offer you some money so you can marry the daughter of a wealthy family. By this means, everyone can be satisfied.

CHANG: If I do not have Little Nightingale, what use have I for your money? I shall henceforth satisfy myself with the beauty found in books. I go.

MOTHER: Stay. You have drunk quite a bit today. Red Maid, see Elder Brother to the study. I will talk to you further tomorrow, Master Chang. (She leaves.)

RED MAID: You should not have drunk so much.

CHANG (going to his knees in front of Red Maid): What have I come to? Because of your Young Mistress I have paid no attention to food or sleep, feeling as though I had lost something which I then found.

After my first glimpse of her and, then, the verses in the garden, I have been able to think of nothing else. And now, this unfortunate turn of events. I feel completely helpless. Would you be good enough to tell your Young Mistress that there is nothing else I can do?

And now, I am going to hang myself with my belt, in front of you.

RED MAID: Why do that? I have a plan.

CHANG: What is it? Quickly!

RED MAID: I noticed that you have a lute on which I am certain you are very adept. My Young Mistress is very fond of the lute, too, so listen.

Tonight I will take my Young Mistress out into the garden near your window to burn some joss sticks. When you hear me cough, start playing and I will then tell Little Nightingale what you just told me now. If she has anything to say, I will let you know.

Now I must go. I'm afraid the Old Mistress will be looking for me.

"You have drunk quite a bit today."

PART II

ACT V

Scene 1. The Western Chamber that evening

CHANG (aside): It grows dark so slowly. What does it
it take to make the time pass more quickly. Oh
Moon! Can you not come out earlier tonight?

(Addressing his lute): We have been through many sea-
sons together, old friend — to places great and
small. I'm depending on you for my success in
this matter.

Lend me a gentle breeze, O Heaven, to float the
sound of my lute to those ears of powdered jade.

(Little Nightingale appears in the garden followed by Red
Maid.)

RED MAID: What a brilliant moon! You can burn the
joss sticks over here, Mistress.

LITTLE NIGHTINGALE: Why burn incense when everything has ended in failure? O Moon, you are round
and whole, but what about me?

The fragile blossoms scattered across the steps
may be fragrant and beautiful but they are no
longer alive; death follows every separation. Who
says that a good beginning has a good ending?

To me he has turned from a lover into a mirage;
to him I have become a vision without substance.
All I can do from now on is hold him in my heart
and see him in my dreams. My lips will do nothing
more than speak of him.

74

Today, my thoughts danced about a grand and joyous wedding. When my mother told me to offer him a jade cup full of wine, I thought in my confused excitement that it was a sign of her great affection for him. Instead, it was her way of turning me into his sister, making marriage impossible.

RED MAID: There is a halo around the moon. It will probably be windy tomorrow.

LITTLE NIGHTINGALE: The Goddess of the Moon is surrounded by a dense cloud for fear that her heart might be moved to love. When I see her unaccompanied and alone, as she is tonight, I feel displeased with the Lord of Heaven.

(Red Maid coughs and Chang begins to play on his lute.)

LITTLE NIGHTINGALE: What is that sound?

RED MAID: What sound?

LITTLE NIGHTINGALE: Is it the tinkling of head ornaments or the bells on a skirt as it sweeps along? Is it the wind chimes under the eaves or the rings on a loose curtain caught by the breeze?

Hush! It is the sound of the lute coming from the Western Chamber, as masculine as the sabre and spear of a warrior horseman.

Now it is gentle like flowers falling onto a stream; now it soars like the cry of a crane in the clear moonlit air. And now it is low, like the whisper of lovers at the window.

He plays with such intensity; I know what he is thinking. His song is that of the male phoenix bemoaning the loss of the female and I cannot help from being aroused. I must go nearer.

RED MAID: I will be back in a moment. I am going to see what your mother is doing.

CHANG (aside): There is someone outside the window. It must be Little Nightingale. I'll play ' The Courtship of The Phoenix ' and hope it does for me what it did for the Scholar Su Ma when he was pursuing the beautiful Wen Chun.

> So fair this beautiful lady,
> To see her was not to forget,
> To see her and not see her often
> Filled even the proud with regret.
>
> The phoenix soars over the ocean,
> Traversing its length and breadth,
> Its timeless search for a lover
> Ending only in merciful death.

Alas, she is not in the garden! My lute speaks my love far better than my poor words, but where is she? When are our hands to find each other? If I cannot be with her forever, let me die.

LITTLE NIGHTINGALE (to herself): He plays well but his song is sad. My eyes are filled with tears.

Word after word falls as gently as the rain, sound after sound with the sadness of a life that is wasting away. The sorrow in his music makes me love him even more.

CHANG (Aside, still unaware that Little Nightingale is outside his window): And you, young lady; do you also deceive me with your looks and words?

LITTLE NIGHTINGALE (hears him but still speaks softly to

...e Nightingale listening to Scholar Chang playing the lute.

herself): How can you say that? How unjust! This strategy was my mother's, not mine. I am not allowed to seek a lover like a phoenix. I am kept at my needlework night and day without a moment for myself. She cares not about my happiness.

Only a single sheet of rice paper across the window separates us; there are no clouded mountains rising between us, peak after peak, and yet I can find no way to let you know how I feel.

RED MAID (rushing to Little Nightingale hurriedly): Quickly! Your mother is looking for you. We had better go in.

LITTLE NIGHTINGALE (aside): She comes in such a flurry, with no regard for my condition, giving me such a fright. Why does this child speak so loud that all can hear?

Would that I could stay a while longer but should I delay, my mother may discover what has been happening here. And that would be the end of me.

RED MAID: Still anxious to hear more of the lute, are you, Mistress? Scholar Chang has asked me to tell you he is leaving.

LITTLE NIGHTINGALE: Oh, no! He must wait a little longer. Tell him to stay.

RED MAID: What am I to say?

LITTLE NIGHTINGALE: Say that my mother has something to tell him and that he will not go away empty-handed.

PART III

ACT I

Scene 1. Little Nightingale's room in the Western Chamber the next morning

LITTLE NIGHTINGALE (to herself): After hearing the lute last night, I am more uneasy than before. I'll ask Red Maid to find out how he is today.

Red Maid?!

RED MAID: Elder Sister. What can I do for you?

LITTLE NIGHTINGALE: You know I have not been feeling well. Why have you not come to see me? I have something for you to do. Look in on Scholar Chang and see how he is today.

RED MAID: Me? If your mother found out she would not like it.

LITTLE NIGHTINGALE: Good Sister. I beg you to do this for me.

(She goes to her knees.)

RED MAID: Please get up. Please. I will go to see him.

(She begins to leave.)

I will say: 'Master Chang, your illness is the same as that of my mistress. The powder and rouge have disappeared from her face and she has not the heart to continue her needlework. The only cure is to see each other heart-to-heart.'

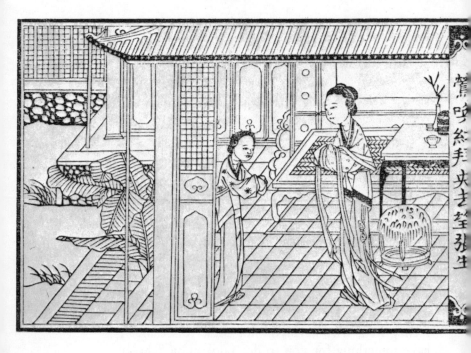

"Look in on Scholar Chang and see how he is today."

Scene 2. The study of the Western Chamber

CHANG (Aside, lying on the couch in the study of the Western Chamber where he has been since the dinner): This is killing me. The day wears on and there is still no word from Little Nightingale. I have asked the Superior to say I am sick in bed but no one has come to see me. If only I could get some sleep..

RED MAID (Aside, on her way to Chang's room): The handsome scholar is filled with confusion and tears smear the powder of the beautiful maid. He grows grey and she grows thin. One is sleepless but too tired to read and the other is too dejected to pick

80

Maid knocks on Scholar Chang's door with her golden hair pin.

up her needle and thread. He plays his lute with mechanical fingers while she tries to complete a verse for a broken heart. They are victims of the same illness.

(Outside Chang's window): Now, if I wet the corner of the paper covering the window and lift it just a bit like this, I will be able to see what he is doing.

There he is, lying in bed with his clothes on, looking so forlorn and miserable. How pale he is!

You look like you are dying of love, Scholar Chang, although it could be that you are just bored to death.

81

(She knocks on the door with her golden hair ornament.)

CHANG: Who's there?

RED MAID: It is the evil spirit of the five plagues, spreading a sickness called love. My Young Mistress sent me.

CHANG: How is she?

RED MAID: She has had no time for powder and rouge today and yet has already had a thousand thoughts of a certain great scholar.

CHANG: I want to send her a letter. Can you deliver it for me?

RED MAID: If I do, I know that my Mistress will be beside herself with delight. But she will pull a long face and say: ' Red Maid! Who gave you this letter? How dare you bring me a letter from someone I barely know, you little minx!' Then, without reading it, she will tear it up and it will fall to the floor in a thousand pieces.

CHANG: I am certain she will not do that. You just don't want to deliver the letter for me. But if you do, Red Maid, I will give you some money.

RED MAID: You wretched, vulgar creature! Don't try to show me how rich you are. Do you think I came here to see what I could get from you? All the money you make from your wretched teaching wouldn't be enough to buy me.

Do you think I really want your money?

Do you think that people can be swayed as easily as the branch of a plum tree in the spring wind? Or purchased like those who stand in the doorways along the streets? I may be only a mere serving-maid but I have my pride. If you said, as you should, 'Have pity on me, a poor and lonely man,' I would have considered the matter.

CHANG: Come, Red Maid. Have pity on my misery. I'll say whatever you wish.

RED MAID: All right. Go ahead and write your letter and I'll take it to her.

(Chang writes in a rapid flowing hand, without hesitation.)

RED MAID: How nice you write! May I know what you say in the letter?

CHANG (reads): A hundred bows. Since I saw you last, we have neither met, spoken nor written, and I am miserable. Who would have expected your mother to break her word and turn my gratitude into a complaint?

I am now confined to the other side of the wall, yearning to be in your bed chamber. I think of you unceasingly and am despondent, awaiting my end.

As Red Maid is here, I take the liberty of asking her to bring you these few words to show my heart's poor condition. If you would be considerate enough to reply, even a few words would keep me alive.

Please forgive my taking this liberty and accept these five-character lines:

> Mutual longings double the loneliness,
> Sadness strums the white-jade lute;
> Happy thoughts are springtime's confection
> Arousing our hearts to pursuit.
>
> Resist not my fiery passion,
> Respect not the hollow restraints;

張生央紅娘遞緘與鶯鶯

"I want to send her a letter. Can you deliver it for me?"

> Refuse not the moon's invitation
> To joining in shadowy plaints.

RED MAID: I expected you to draft the letter slowly and carefully, but you have written it with a running pen, ending it with a perceptive eight-line verse and skilfully folding it into a lovers' knot. It is very clever and exceedingly thoughtful, with strong sentiments. If your love is a mere pretence, you conceal it with convincing words, leading me to believe that you are as careful as you are thoughtful.

When she reads it, I must watch her face closely
to see whether it causes anger or joy.

(Chang hands her the letter.)

RED MAID: I am only too pleased to deliver it for
you.

You have a hand that can pluck a woman as
easily as a flower, but you must also be able to
pluck an important position with a well-written
examination. Don't let your wings become en-
tangled in the threads of love; don't let the golden
nightingale stay the lofty flight of the falcon. You
must not, because of a beautiful woman, fail to
attain the highest honours in the Examination.

CHANG: Thank you for your concern.

RED MAID: Leave everything to me.

(Begins to leave.)

RED MAID (to herself): Since that first exchange of
glances revealed in full their love, I have thought
night and day on how to bring about this match.
How could I neglect a letter as important as this? I
will not only deliver it but, with my own tongue,
will speak the sentiments of love contained therein.

I will arrange for her to visit you, Scholar Chang;
leave it to me.

(She leaves.)

CHANG: There is nothing left to do but wait.

PART III

ACT II

Scene 1. Little Nightingale's room

LITTLE NIGHTINGALE (Aside, in bed): Red Maid has been busy with my mother all morning. I'm so tired I shall sleep a little longer.

RED MAID (Aside, entering): Ah, she is still asleep. The air is clam and the fragrance of flowers floats through the window. Her lamp still burns, throwing its silver light on her lilies of gold as I draw aside the net around her bed.

How languid she looks, her hair in clouds of disarray. The sun is high and still her eyes stay shut.

Ah, she stirs a little and scratches her ear; and now, a deep sigh as she begins to sit. If I show her the letter, I am afraid she will pretend to be too shy to accept it. I had better leave it on her dressing table.

(Little Nightingale moves to her dressing table, looks in the mirror and begins to arrange her hair.)

RED MAID (aside): She sees it now and opens the envelope. She reads it intently. And then reads it again. And again. And now, she begins to look displeased. And now, suddenly, her fair face turns to me in anger.

LITTLE NIGHTINGALE (shouting angrily): Red Maid! Red Maid!

(Red Maid, her face turned away, does not answer.)

LITTLE NIGHTINGALE: You shameful trollop! Where are you?

RED MAID   (aside): The game is up.

LITTLE NIGHTINGALE: You have become a procuress now, have you? Where does this come from? I am the daughter of a Prime Minister. Who dares insult my virtue with a letter such as this? Never, never have I seen anything like it. Let me tell my mother and you shall have a good thrashing.

RED MAID: It was you, Mistress, who sent me to him and he who sent me back with this letter. How could I have dared ask him for it? How would I know what he wrote when I cannot read?

You are responsible, not I. Here I am caught between two love-sick people and now I am the one who is guilty. This may not be your way of doing things, but it is not mine either.

Please don't make such a big thing of this, Mistress. Just give the letter to your mother. Or do you want me to give it to her?

(She takes the letter and starts toward the door.)

LITTLE NIGHTINGALE: Come back here.

RED MAID: Why?

LITTLE NIGHTINGALE: It's not important. How's Master Chang today?

RED MAID: Why?

LITTLE NIGHTINGALE: Come, Little Sister. Tell me.

RED MAID: I cannot bear to look at him: he has become so pale and thin. He has not only forgotten his meals but has abandoned sleep, thinking of you day and night. Looking constantly in this direction, his eyes are glazed with tears.

LITTLE NIGHTINGALE: A doctor should be called to find out what his ailment is.

RED MAID: His sickness cannot be cured with medicine. He is feverish and can be cured only with love.

LITTLE NIGHTINGALE: Master Chang and I are Brother and Sister, nothing more. Thank heaven you are as discreet as you are, Little Sister. If others knew of this, what would they say?

RED MAID: Whom are you trying to deceive, Mistress? This situation has become so confused, who knows what is really happening?

Do you care if his condition is serious or not? You encourage him to climb to dangerous heights and then take the ladder away and regard his plight with indifference.

LITTLE NIGHTINGALE: Get me a pen. I'll write and tell him he must not take such liberties again. (She begins to write.) When you take this to him, Red Maid, tell him that I regard him as a Brother and nothing else. And that if he writes a letter like this again I shall tell my mother, and he and you both will be held to account.

(She gives the letter to Red Maid.)

RED MAID (aside): I do not understand you, Mistress. That first night in the garden, you complained that your garments were too thin to keep out the cold. But on the night you heard the lute, when the moon sparkled the heavy dew, you said nothing of the cold. Was it because you were feeling the hot breath of passion?

Did you not feel ashamed then? If he means nothing to you, Mistress, why do you look so longingly for him through the window, like the faithful wife who was turned to stone by Heaven? Are you, too, afraid he is lost?

I have been ready from the start of this affair to act as the bearer of your missives, without criticizing the rashness and folly of it. And now, you are only too ready to put the blame on me.

You are not fooling anyone. You may casually call him 'Elder Brother' in front of everyone but when you are alone, your eyes are sad with tears.

I shouldn't deliver this letter, but if I don't, you will criticize me again, this time for disobeying your orders. Still, I wouldn't deliver it if Scholar Chang were not waiting for a reply.

Scene 2.   The study

(Red Maid knocks.)

CHANG (opening door): Red Maid! The only pillar left to keep the sky from falling in on me. You have her answer?

RED MAID: It is all over.

CHANG: My letter was an invitation to a rendezvous. It is apparent that you did not care enough to help.

RED MAID: So, I get it from you too, do I? That was a very nice letter you wrote. Blame your luck, not my neglect. That letter was not only your confession but your death warrant. If my Mistress had not been understanding and considerate, I would have been held equally guilty.

Your chances of seeing Little Nightingale again, except as a brother, are gone. It is very unlikely that the moon will shine on the Western Chamber for you again.

You go your way, Elder Brother, and let my Mistress go hers. There is nothing else for us to do but disappear like the guests after a banquet.

I'm afraid the Old Mistress will be looking for me. I must go.

CHANG: Once you have gone, I am finished. You must do one more favour to try and save my life.

(He takes her hands and kneels in front of her.)

RED MAID: You are a very learned man, Scholar Chang. Do you not see how the matter stands? Don't try to pretend. You want this love affair so badly, you do not mind if I get a thrashing in the process. The old woman has a rod heavy and thick enough to break every bone in my body.

Let me go. I have already risked too much on your behalf.

CHANG (still holding on to her hands and beginning to weep): There is nothing left for me to do. You are my only hope. My life depends on you.

RED MAID: I don't know why I listen to you when you make life so difficult. Here is the answer to your letter. Read it yourself.

CHANG (reading letter): I don't believe it. How is it

possible ... that such a thing could happen? This calls for the burning of incense and prayers of thanks. Had I known this letter was coming, I could have prepared myself for it. Are you not pleased, little maid?

RED MAID: About what?

CHANG: This is my most fortunate day.

RED MAID: What are you talking about?

CHANG: Your Mistress puts on her anger like a mask. Her true feelings are quite different. She wants me to meet her in the garden tonight.

RED MAID: This cannot be true. Read the letter to me.

CHANG: 'When the moon is over the Western Chamber,
And the wind sets the door ajar,
Watch for the shadows on the wall to move,
The jade flower will not be far'.

It is quite clear to me that she wants me to wait in the garden for her tonight.

RED MAID: And it is quite clear to me that you are making all this up. Are you sure that is the meaning?

CHANG: How can I make a mistake about something like this? I am an expert at riddles. Look here. The second line means she is going to open the door and, in the third line, she says she is going to walk among the flowers near the wall. The ' jade flower ' in the last line is she.

RED MAID (aside): Never have I been so thoroughly made a fool of. You may be young, Mistress, but you are exceedingly clever, leading me to think you regard him as an Elder Brother as you use me to arrange the time and place for a secret meeting in some lonely corner.

Your letter paper, smooth and white, has the fragrance of orchid and musk but I also detect a fragrance that is yours alone and see where the tears have fallen.

Your letter has all the melancholy of spring about it. It should set this learned scholar's mind at ease to know that he now can obtain, at will, possession of the one who wears a golden bird in her hair.

You have come to abuse me so easily and give him your affection so readily, I am beginning to wonder just when you began to play the loyal wife.

With him you use honeyed words that would warm one even in December but for me the words are harsh and chilling even in June.

Now let's see what your next step is going to be.

CHANG: How am I to get over the wall to her garden?

RED MAID: That is your problem. If you are worried about a low wall, how will you ever hurdle the Examination? If you have difficulties when alone in a garden of gentle flowers, how will you wrestle the scholastic laurels from all those who strive for them at the Capital?

Make haste and have no fear. Her eyes yearn like the dark ripples of autumn; her eyebrows, as delicate as the hills of spring, turn up with longing.

CHANG: Perhaps. But we have been together in the garden twice so far and nothing happened either time.

RED MAID: This will not be like any other time. The promise is in your hands.

CHANG: All of life is predestined. And unpredictable. Now that I have shown how expert I am at finding my way through poetic riddles, how do I find a way over the wall without making a fool of myself?

(He goes to the window and looks out.)

Move, sun, move. You have an eternity ahead of you. Why be so stingy with one day? Why do you stay rooted in the sky?

(He paces the study and then looks out again.)

How can the sun still be so high? Is it afraid to go down because a legendary hero in need of light for a battle is shaking his spear at it?

(He paces the floor and looks out again.)

How is it that the Three-Legged Golden Crow* is still there? How can I get the arrow of Hou Yi* to shoot it down?

Ring the evening bells, brothers! The willow branch will help me over the wall.

*References to legends about the sun.

PART III

ACT III

Scene 1. The garden

RED MAID (aside, in the doorway of Little Nightingale's room):
Since my young mistress has decided not to confide
in me, I won't reveal how much I know. Then we
shall see how clever she is when she tries to get
away for her secret meeting. (Aloud to Little Nightingale): Elder Sister, let us go out into the garden
and light some joss sticks.

(They both go out.)

LITTLE NIGHTINGALE:
> The fragrance of flowers fills the night;
> Deep in the garden, the moon shines bright.

RED MAID (aside): How beautiful! The setting sun
paints the pavilion in the vermillion of my mistress's
blush as the flowers release love's fragrance on the
evening breeze. The noise and bustle of the day
subside as the crows hide themselves in the pale
willow and the ducks find quiet sleep on the pond's
green mirror.

The beauty and the scholar can scarcely wait for
the night to unite them under its dark cover. The
time passes as slowly as a hot summer as they wait
for the sun to drop behind the willows and then
slip behind the distant hills. They would not mind
if it disappeared forever on this night.

Bewitching in her gossamer gown, she is as restless

as the birds in spring. Once shy and reticent, her longing has overcome her sense of propriety.

(To Little Nightingale): The gate is open, Mistress. I had better close it lest someone intrude.

(As she goes to close the gate which leads into the garden, she sees someone outside and can barely recognize him in the gathering darkness.)

(Aside): The black silk hat of the scholar can almost be mistaken for a crow in this light. But it is he, trying to conceal himself while she stands hidden from him by that large rock.

CHANG (coming toward the figure he sees in the dark):   You are here. I have waited so long; this moment has come too quickly.

(He timidly attempts to take her in his arms.)

RED MAID: You beast, it is I! Be more careful. Suppose I had been the Old Mistress? I know you are so excited with passion that you cannot see straight but you'd better look before you jump next time.

Are you certain she meant that you should come?

CHANG: I am so smitten I cannot see clearly. Where is Little Nightingale?

RED MAID: On the other side of the rock. Are you sure she asked you to come?

CHANG: I already told you I am an expert at poetic riddles. I wouldn't make a mistake like this.

RED MAID: Go back through the gate or she will say that I let you in. You must climb over the wall.

Please do exactly what I say. I am here to help

you two get together. Climb the wall and then make the green moss your embroidered couch. The flowers and weeping willows will be your curtains.

The night grows deep and quiet and a cloud begins to veil the bright moon. The time is now. Be very gentle. This is not a roadside willow or a plucked blossom. This is an innocent young maid whose affections you can win only with sweet caressing words — a delicate flawless jade, fair of face with guileless grace.

I cannot help or advise you beyond this point. You are on your own. Now is the time to end your grief and banish sorrow. Brace yourself and be a man, tender and understanding.

(As he goes out through the gate and starts to climb back over the wall, she says): I take pity on you, my learned friend.

LITTLE NIGHTINGALE: (seeing a dark figure coming over the wall): Who is it?

CHANG: It is I.

LITTLE NIGHTINGALE: What are you up to, Scholar Chang? Here I am burning incense for my poor father and there you are coming over the wall like a thief in the middle of the night. What kind of person are you? If my mother discovered you, how would you explain it?

CHANG (to himself): She has changed her mind again.

RED MAID (aside): A go-between's work is never done when those who say they seek a union continue to differ and quarrel. I listen furtively on tip-toe and what do I hear? One is full of shame and the other

96

is full of anger. One is unable to say a word while the other chatters on endlessly. One's mind is inflexibly set on one goal while the other is constantly changing hers.

What has become of all your bold talk, Master Chang? Get on with it! You are like an embroidered pillow, nice to look at but full of air.

LITTLE NIGHTINGALE: Red Maid! There is an intruder here.

RED MAID: Who is it?

CHANG: It's I, the scholar.

RED MAID: Master Chang, what are you doing here?

LITTLE NIGHTINGALE: Call my mother.

RED MAID: If we called your mother, it could be embarrassing for everyone. Let us take the matter into our own hands. Come over here and kneel down, Scholar Chang. (As he starts to do so, she continues.) As a student of Confucius, you must know the principles of propriety.

Why have you come here at this late hour? What were your intentions? Your knowledge may be as deep as the sea but your audacity is as unlimited as the sky.

We do not want to be your judges, so how do you plead? Guilty or not guilty?

CHANG: What harm have I done?

RED MAID: Who invited you here? You are supposed to be at the Capital reaching for the laurels at the Examination, not here trying to steal the most beautiful flower in the garden.

Why don't you go on to the Imperial Examination and, as they say, 'leap over the Dragon's Gate', instead of riding the galloping horse of seduction over our wall?

Ah, well. Forgive this poor fellow, Elder Sister, for my sake, if for nothing else.

LITTLE NIGHTINGALE: I still think I should call my mother. If there were a scandal, how would you face your relatives and friends, Master Chang?

All right, get up, please.

RED MAID: Thank you, Mistress, for your wisdom and kindness. (To Chang): You may be a learned scholar but what would you do if we reported this to the magistrate?

LITTLE NIGHTINGALE: You should be rewarded for saving our lives, but this is hardly the way to behave toward a Younger Sister. If it happens again, you will not be let off so easily.

(She leaves.)

CHANG (looking toward the departing Little Nightingale): But . . . but you told me to come.

RED MAID (mockingly): For shame! For shame! What happened to all your big talk about unquenchable passion and consuming love?

CHANG: I can only accept what destiny offers.

RED MAID: Never talk again about a spring evening worth ten thousand pieces of gold. Prepare to spend another ten years looking through a bachelor's cold window.

The past master of poetic riddles has miscounted the beats in the line about the wind pushing the door open. The moon has gone behind the clouds and the wall has turned into an impasse.

Primp and preen as much as you will, Scholar Chang. The trouble you take with your appearance is touching, but she will not be touched, at least not by such an artless bungler as you.

What a farce this has become! The great storm cloud threatens with lightning and thunder but not a single drop of water falls to relieve the drought.

Forget your gallant speeches, learned one, and pen no more seductive verses. You are still an amateur in the art of romance. Go back to your studies.

And you, Young Mistress, no longer have any right to feign anger or sadness. It is all finished.

(She leaves.)

CHANG (looking at Red Maid as she leaves): Your Mistress has taken care of me nicely. I can put the foolish thoughts of romance out of my mind, but what will I do about this yearning in my heart? How do I get rid of that?

I'd better get back to my room.

PART III

ACT IV

Scene 1. Little Nightingale's room, the following morning

RED MAID: The Superior told your mother this morning that Master Chang is very ill. He did not look very well when he left here last night. You have done it this time, Mistress.

LITTLE NIGHTINGALE: I have already heard about the poor man. I have a cure for him in this letter. Please take it to him.

RED MAID: Here we go again. Please do not make matters worse, Mistress.

LITTLE NIGHTINGALE: Go, good Sister. You will be saving his life.

(She exits.)

Scene 2. The study, where Chang is lying down

CHANG (aside): Last night was such a catastrophe. My old ailment has returned and I feel quite helpless. The old mistress has sent for a doctor but this illness is not something a doctor can cure. What I need is a fragrant drop of nectar from the tongue of Little Nightingale.

RED MAID (entering): I am certain this prescription is going to aggravate his illness. If medicine cannot cure the sickness one gets when parted from one's home country, how can it cure the sickness one gets when parted from one's true love?

The way I am being used like a needle and thread is becoming annoying. Back and forth, back and forth, without end. Why not let things happen as they will? Distant seas and elusive peaks are unattainable.

(She approaches Chang): I am so sorry for you, Master Chang. How are you?

CHANG: Should I die, young Miss, please be my witness before the final judge at the gates of eternity. I have not been false.

RED MAID: Many in this mixed-up world suffer from heart-ache but not as seriously as this. I am sure my Mistress does not realize what she is doing.

CHANG: This is my reward for saving her.

RED MAID: But she is not completely to blame. You and your unbridled passion are as much responsible for your being reduced to skin and bones. And now, you are not only battering your head against an insurmountable wall of refusal but are forgetting your future in the Capital.

Oh yes, my Mistress has asked me to come and see what medicine you have and offers another remedy.

CHANG: What is it?

RED MAID: Here.

CHANG (reading it, he stands up and begins to smile): If I knew you were bringing this letter, I would have come out to greet your arrival with joy.

RED MAID: Now what! This is the second time.

CHANG: The meaning of this letter is quite clear. She is really expecting me this time.

RED MAID: You are a silly fool! A mad bookworm! You don't know the first thing about love and here you are finding all kinds of hidden meanings in what people write. What does the letter say? Read it to me.

CHANG (reading): It says, ' Be not troubled with the trifles of the past. Do not let the talents given by Heaven be destroyed. I did not realize how much mischief my maidenly modesty would cause. In order to repay your great kindness, it is no longer possible to act with propriety. Tonight, without fail, the fragile cloud will move before the strong wind.'

This letter cannot be compared with that of yesterday. I am certain she will come.

RED MAID: And what will happen if she does? It is not enough to have a small coverlet with a lute for a pillow. She will shiver from the cold.

CHANG: Here are ten taels of silver. Can you get something with that?

RED MAID: In the garden last night, every minute would have been worth a thousand taels of gold.

I have pillows embroidered with birds of love and a silk coverlet of turquoise which would win the heart of any romantic young woman. But how can I lend them to you? How could she do anything under her maid's covers?

Perhaps it will be better if you do not undress. It

would be better than nothing at all. If your love is
finally realized, what need is there for fancy
pillows?

When you see her eyes, as dark as the seas of
autumn, and her milk-white skin — when you
touch her waist, as pliant as a young willow, and
see how beautiful she is, you will forget your past
troubles.

As lovely as she is to look at, it is her inner
beauty which will captivate you — her tender
heart, her kind manners, and her gentle nature.

She needs nothing more to cure you, neither
magical powers nor divine remedies. She herself
will be enough.

Still . . . I doubt if she will come. How can she at
such a late hour?

CHANG: Do not concern yourself with the how or the
when. Just do your best to help me.

RED MAID: I have never done anything but my best
for you . . . and it was never with the thought of
jade or gold as a reward. All I want is a head
covered with flowers and a long embroidered gown
for the wedding.

CHANG: But what if the old woman does keep her in?
Then what?

RED MAID: Don't worry. Should the Old Mistress
shut tight the door, I will arrange something sooner
or later. I'll do my best for you; just do your best
for yourself.

When you see Little Nightingale, do not allow
consent or refusal to rest with her. This night is in
your hands.

103

PART IV

ACT I

Scene 1. Little Nightingale's room, later that night

LITTLE NIGHTINGALE: Red Maid, get my bed ready. I am going to sleep.

RED MAID: What do you mean you are going to sleep? What about the scholar?

LITTLE NIGHTINGALE: What about him?

RED MAID: Mistress! You cannot do this! If you change your mind again, I am going to tell your mother that you wrote a letter to arrange a secret meeting with Master Chang.

LITTLE NIGHTINGALE: How can I go? The very idea frightens me.

RED MAID: What is there to be shy about? When you get there, close your eyes. Come, let us be off.

LITTLE NIGHTINGALE: My mother will hear us.

RED MAID: She is already in bed. Let us go. Quickly!

LITTLE NIGHTINGALE (not moving): I cannot . . .

RED MAID: Quickly! Come!

(Little Nightingale begins to move hesitantly toward the door.)

RED MAID (aside): My mistress's words are stubborn but her feet are giving in.

How pure and beautiful she has been, in endless thought of her poet prince from one day to the next, morning till night. And now, about to make up for all the broken promises and crushed hopes

104

Part Four   Act One

of the past, she leaves her pillow for his, for her
first lesson in the ancient art of love. It is the story
of the Fairy of Love and the Prince of Chu all over
again.

(To Nightingale): Wait a moment, Mistress.

LITTLE NIGHTINGALE:

Come, sister, I'm ready, don't wait for the moon.
Come, sister, what keeps you? Come quickly,
      come soon.
I long to see my lute-player fair,
And hope that the monks are deeply in prayer.
My shoes are snug, my feet are ready,
With graceful movements, light and steady,
To travel softly with nary a word
To arouse a sly suspecting bird.

RED MAID (rejoining Little Nightingale):

The long, long journey begins its end
These pillows and covers make me bend,
The candle casts its quiet light,
And now comes the moon to start the night.
The embroidered covers fragrant with musk,
The pillows' warmth and my mistress's trust
Should bring an end to the long, long wait
But all still lies in the hands of fate.

(They leave.)

Scene 2.   The study

CHANG (aside, standing in the doorway that leads from the
   study to the courtyard): The first gong of the night

watch sounds. Where is she? The night is far advanced and a fragrant mist fills the golden air. Which of the clouds are bringing the news I am waiting to hear?

The light of the moon floods the pavilion and the monks have gone to their lonely prayers, leaving the night to the cawing of the crows in the courtyard.

Each time I see the shadows of the flowers move against the wall, my heart leaps with uncontrollable excitement. Is it she or is it not? Are the sounds I hear her gold ornaments or are they the wind in the bamboos? My eyes strain through the darkness and find nothing to comfort my body or mind. All I can do is lean against this door and wait for whatever it is that is going to emerge from this night.

LITTLE NIGHTINGALE (aside):

> The temple gong tonight sounds deep,
> I hope my mother is fast asleep,
> The chilling wind may pierce my cheek but
> The shrouded moon will hide my secret.
> In the night's deep quiet no one can see
> The path through the garden that carries me
> Under begonias whose petals red
> Anoint me with dew for the tryst ahead.

CHANG (aside): Does she know that I never stop thinking of her? I am so weary and confused, I can no longer keep my eyes open or my thoughts straight. Had I never come to this Monastery I would have been spared the torments of the last few days and nights. It was a mistake, and the only thing to do now is admit it and rectify it. I must now transfer my love of beauty to a love of virtue. But, alas, how can I do anything with my love when she possesses it?

It may be that she is finding it difficult to get away from her mother. Perhaps the one who has imprisoned my heart is herself a prisoner.

My eyes falter and my heart begins to sink. Is she proving false again?

Were she coming, she would have left her room by now and should soon be here to fill this room with joy. But if she is now asleep, I had better cast my heavy hopes into the sea.

LITTLE NIGHTINGALE (aside):
    The moon has climbed the willowed ridge,
    Will fate replay the sad Blue Bridge?
    What will he wear? How shall we meet?
    What should I say? Should I be sweet?
    Ten thousand emotions set me a-quiver,
    Like a landed fish who sees the river.
    The moment we meet is the moment I'll treasure,
    Ten thousand taels can't buy this night's pleasure.

CHANG (aside): Perhaps I should write one last letter, just a few brief lines, to say:
    'Why have you been so cruel to me when I have shown only love for you? From the first meeting of our eyes to the last of the broken promises, my feelings have grown until they can no longer be endured.

    'I eat and drink only enough to keep alive and am ready to put up with all manner of abuse and

107

trickery because I love you. I have suffered so much and so long in keeping my heart patient and my body alive, it would take six months to tally all my sorrows and ten carts to carry my grief.'

RED MAID (with Little Nightingale in the corridor leading to the door on the other side of the study): Wait here, Mistress, while I go ahead.

(She knocks.)

CHANG: Who is it?

RED MAID: Your fairy godmother.

CHANG (opening the door and seeing only Red Maid): Is your Mistress with you?

RED MAID: She is coming. Here, take the coverlet and pillows. How are you going to thank me for this, Scholar Chang?

CHANG: Sister, no words can express my gratitude. At this moment, only Heaven knows what is in my heart.

RED MAID: Gently, gently, or you will frighten her. Wait. (She goes back to where Little Nightingale is waiting.): Go ahead, Elder Sister. I will wait for you here.

CHANG (seeing Little Nightingale come into the room, he goes to his knees and puts his arms around her waist): This can only be a dream. How can it be otherwise? How do I deserve a visit from the Princess of Heaven?

(Little Nightingale's head and eyes are downcast and she does not look at or speak to Chang.)

CHANG: I am a stranger in a strange land, with neither grace, looks nor talent, a clumsy admirer sick with love. How could I dare hope that you would take pity on me and come to cure this fatal illness?

(He leads Nightingale to the couch, unable to take his eyes from her. As they sit, she keeps silent, her head and eyes still cast down.)

CHANG: Delicate embroidered shoes, only half the size of mine; a willowy waist that one hand can enfold; a lovely face overcome with shyness, unable to look into mine.

Gently now, your head on my pillow where the love birds flutter in joy. Now the golden hairpins and your hair is free. You are even more beautiful than I had imagined in my sleepless torment.

And now the belt and the buttons. How still you are! Do you know how completely you have enslaved me? Why do you not look at me? Why are you so quiet?

My arms find you soft, warm and fragrant; and I am in paradise. It is spring and the jade flower is in the fullness of bloom.

Under the faint glow of the lamp, I begin to glimpse the swell of a breast, so pure and full, and below it a waist of willow, soft and trembling. You are so exquisite, I know not where your loveliness begins.

I love you with all my heart and soul and am stunned by your virgin purity but desire overcomes my hesitation.

Together on this cloud of bliss,
Unable to hide my happiness,
I tie your belt in a lovers' knot,

This night of love to be not forgot.
Never.

I kiss your sweet fragrant cheeks; and as the heart of the flower is gently brushed, its petals open with drops of dew. And then I begin to know the indescribable joy of a fish in a quivering stream, of a butterfly fluttering in rapture from the sweet nectar of newly-opened buds. How could I anticipate such bliss after all the bitterness and sorrow?

> A new perfume comes from the covers,
> The perfume of united lovers.
> I vow to you, O mountain and sea,
> This love will be for eternity.
> Forever.

My happiness mounts, my soul flies to the highest heaven. To heaven! Heaven!

Ah, joy, so complete but still unreal. Has it really happened? The dew falls on the fragrant earth and a blessed mist begins to envelop me. Was this union only a dream or have we really met, sweet lady, so full of love?

RED MAID (knocking softly and calling in a hushed voice): Young Mistress. Please. We had better return.

CHANG: Not yet. Surely not yet.

> The night deepens and my heart now fills
> With dreams of joy that circle the hills.
> Let the unknown future its cold wind bring,
> Under this cover it is warm as spring.
> My illness is ended, I am ready to leap,
> Wakened at last from my tortured sleep,

But she leaves me, my bride, my flower so fair,
She returns to her gown and re-does her hair.

RED MAID: Mistress! Hurry! It is late!

CHANG: And now the sad inevitable parting. How full this brief moment was, how perfect! When I look at you I am bewitched; when you are gone, my heart is going to be troubled.

LITTLE NIGHTINGALE: I must go. My mother will be looking for me.

CHANG (taking Little Nightingale's hands in his): The fragrant belt that has kept you from me now ties our hearts together. When are we to untie it again?

RED MAID (opening door): Quickly, Elder Sister! We must go back.

(She looks at Chang): You lucky man! But I am happy for you both.

(Chang reluctantly lets Little Nightingale's hands slip out of his and, as the two women leave through the door leading to the courtyard, he stands looking after them.)

CHANG (aside): She said nothing, yet her murmurs told me everything; so lovely, she makes everything else pale. I feel so unworthy and yet become impatient for tomorrow. She must come.

Slowly she slips away through the mist and my heart falters. But she too seems to falter as she floats across the green moss into the night.

What is this on the steps? A pure white silk handkerchief, with a touch of red. I feel so unworthy.

PART IV

ACT II

Scene 1. The Western Chamber, one month later

MOTHER: I have begun to notice during the past few weeks that Little Nightingale spends most of her time dreaming and talks as though her mind were elsewhere. She even seems to walk differently, all of which makes me feel uneasy.

Have you seen Elder Sister, Happy Boy?

HAPPY BOY: She has gone into the garden with Red Maid again. What do they do there every night outside the study? When I go out they always chase me inside.

MOTHER: So that's it. Tell Red Maid to come here at once. Quickly now.

HAPPY BOY (going out to where Little Nightingale and Red Maid are in the garden, speaks to Red Maid): My mother wants you. She knows what you two do every night and is going to give you a good thrashing.

RED MAID: You go ahead, Young Master, and I will follow. I am afraid, Elder Sister, that the game is up. We have been found out. What am I going to do?

LITTLE NIGHTINGALE: Good Sister, protect yourself as best you can. I will tell only what I have to.

RED MAID: It is always thus. When the moon is round and full, the dark clouds cover it; when the flowers are in blossom, it always storms.

You go by night and return by dawn thinking your joy can last forever because you wish it. Why do you stay for the entire night every night, from the rising of the moon to the fading of the morning star?

Your mother is so clever and shrewd, no words of mine will conceal the truth. She must have guessed by now that this broken-down scholar has made himself her son-in-law. And that I, the humble maid, was the matchmaker.

It shows not only in your face but in your figure. The slender melancholy willow is no longer so slender or quite so melancholy. The wasting affliction has been replaced by a vitality and cheerfulness that cannot be disguised.

LITTLE NIGHTINGALE: When you see my mother, be careful what you say.

RED MAID: It is what she is going to say to me that has me worried. She is going to say: 'You little wretch! I order you to watch her carefully and, instead, you are the one who leads her astray.'

What can I say in my defence? I will have to tell her that I never intended to deceive her and make a clean breast of the entire affair.

But you must take all the responsibility for it, Elder Sister, since you got all the joy. What did I get out of it? You enjoy yourselves like love-birds, frolicking to the full, while I wait outside on the damp moss till my feet freeze to ice, afraid to even cough. And now my tender skin will suffer the blows of a thick rod. What profit has there been in

篤篤央囑紅娘夫人前飾非

Little Nightingale begs Red Maid to cover up for her.

this for the miserable go-between?

Wait here, Mistress, and let me go first. I may be able to explain the whole thing to her satisfaction, but don't get your hopes too high. If I fail, on the other hand, don't be too downhearted.

(She goes in to see Little Nightingale's mother.)

MOTHER: You little serpent! Why aren't you down on your knees after what you have done?

RED MAID: I have done nothing.

MOTHER: Wretch! Not only guilty but stubborn! If you do not tell me the truth, I will beat it out of

114

you. Who gave you and Little Nightingale per-
mission to go out at night?

RED MAID: Who says we went out?

MOTHER: Happy Boy saw you. Do you deny it?

(She begins to hit her with a cane rod.)

RED MAID: Stop! Stop! Please stop! I will tell you
everything! (The beating stops but Red Maid continues
to sob.) One night when we were sitting doing
nothing, having finished our sewing and embroidery,
and chatting about nothing in particular, I men-
tioned that Elder Brother was ill, so we decided to
go to the study to see how he was.

MOTHER: And what did you see? What did he say?

RED MAID: His betrayal, he said, had suddenly turned
his happiness to grief. As we began to leave, he told
me to go on ahead first because he had something
to tell Little Nightingale.

MOTHER: She is an unmarried girl. How could you
leave her behind alone?

RED MAID: I thought he wanted her to stay to help
him with his acupuncture needles or with a
moxa-burning treatment. How was I to know they
would end up like the swallows in spring?

They have been with each other every night
since then. I don't know what has happened except
that they have cured each other of their grief and
sorrow and are devoted to each other heart and
soul.

What has happened has happened, Mistress.
They are together and happy. It does no good to

become involved in all the details. When a bird has grown, it becomes more and more difficult to keep it in the nest.

MOTHER: You little whelp! This is all your fault!

RED MAID: It is not my fault, it is not Scholar Chang's fault, and it is not Little Nightingale's fault. It is your fault.

MOTHER: You beast! Are you now accusing me? How is it my fault?

RED MAID: Confucius has said, 'Sincerity is the foundation of life. Without it, nothing is possible. Without axles, how can a cart move?'

When the Monastery was surrounded by brigands, you promised your daughter to whoever succeeded in driving them away. If Master Chang did not love your daughter, do you think he would have offered to help?

Once the danger was past, you changed your mind and went back on your word. Is that the kind of sincerity your life is built on?

When you refused to allow the scholar to marry Little Nightingale, why didn't you just pay him off with gold and ask him to leave? But no! You make matters worse by inviting him to stay in the study near Little Nightingale's room, where he would see her day and night.

That is the cause of all this trouble. If you do not set things right now, it will only make this situation worsen. Not only will the reputation of the family be tarnished but you may suffer even

more should Scholar Chang ever become a pro-
minent official and decide to repay you for this
injury.

If you bring charges against him at this point,
you may find the magistrate inquisitive enough to
uncover your ingratitude. How virtuous would you
appear then?

I do not claim to be right all the time but I beg
that you consider everything before you act. Isn't
it better to forgive a small mistake to avoid a
greater one? When the cost of removing a blemish
is the creation of a lesser blemish, the jade polisher
does not hesitate. Isn't that the better thing to do?

Here are two young people in love. One is a
promising literary light and the other a promising
talent. One is thoroughly versed in the philosophies
and classics and the other is thoroughly adept in
drawing and embroidery. When two young people
like this fall in love, isn't it best to let them follow
their hearts without interfering?

How can you make an enemy of the man who
saved your daughter, and us, from the terror of the
'Flying Tiger'? Do their stars conflict?

It is no longer possible to separate them. And
even if it were, consider the disgrace and dishonour
it would bring the family when the facts became
known.

She is your own flesh and blood, Mistress. Do
not take this matter any further. Let it be.

MOTHER: It is my misfortune to be the mother of
such a disobedient girl. Still, if this case is brought

"Happy Boy saw you. Do you deny it?"

說
合

before the authorities, it will bring great shame to a family whose members have never been guilty of the slightest offence.

It looks, then, that I may have to lose a daughter. Bring the unworthy child here.

RED MAID (returning to Little Nightingale in the garden): The rod forced the truth out of me, Elder Sister. She knows everything and wants to see you immediately.

LITTLE NIGHTINGALE: How can I face her now? I am so embarrassed and ashamed.

RED MAID: What is there to be embarrassed about? She knows all about the birds and the bees.

And when did you begin to feel ashamed? You do not show any shame when you meet your lover each night. It is I who feel embarrassed and ashamed when I see the way the delicate points of your embroidered shoes wriggle when you two are together.

(Little Nightingale, arriving in front of her mother, starts to weep.)

MOTHER (beginning to weep also): My dear child.

(There is an embarrassed silence as they try to collect themselves.)

MOTHER: My dear child. How could you do this to me when I have done my best to bring you up correctly? Did you not stop to think what a great loss of face this would bring — not only for you but for the entire family? If I reported this matter to the magistrate, we would be disgraced.

Who is to blame for this tragic misfortune,

child? Is this my punishment for a sin I committed in an earlier life or a sin you will be punished for in a future life? Is this fate or folly?

It is too late to think of these things now, too late for anything but tears and a try at making the best of a bad situation.

Red Maid, go to the study and bring that beast here.

(Red Maid goes to the study and knocks. Chang opens the door.)

CHANG: Good morning, little maid.

RED MAID: Not as good as you might think, Scholar Chang, and little reason for smiles. Your little affair has been discovered and my Mistress has confessed everything.

You had better come. Her mother wants to see you.

CHANG: How did she find out, and what does she want with me? How can I face her?

RED MAID: You must do it sooner or later. Hide your fear behind a bold face and come. There is no other way. Once she realized what was happening, she made us tell all.

Come, Scholar Chang, do not be afraid to face the old woman. You should be relieved that the matter is now in the open.

Come, Master. Really! You are like a spear made of wax.

(She returns to the Old Mistress followed by the reluctant Chang.)

MOTHER: My good scholar. Have you never heard the

saying: 'What is not considered right by the ancient sages should not be done?'

If I hand you over to the authorities, it will bring great shame to our family's name. If, on the other hand, I give Little Nightingale to you, I will be going against the family tradition of having husbands of official rank for its daughters.

Tomorrow you will proceed to the Capital for the Imperial Examinations. Little Nightingale will remain with me. If you succeed in getting a commission, you may come back for her hand. If you fail, don't bother.

RED MAID   (to herself behind the Old Mistress's back): Oh, Master Chang! I'm so happy for you.

Lift your face and begin to enjoy the love you have had to keep hidden. Who could have hoped for this turn? The future is in your hands. The beauty of this delightful maid is yours if you prove yourself worthy.

MOTHER (to Chang):   Start packing. We will arrange food and wine for your journey and give you a farewell dinner tomorrow at the ten-mile Pavilion of Farewell. Come, daughter.

(She and Little Nightingale leave.)

RED MAID: Just wait till you return. The flutes and drums will fill the wedding hall with joyful sounds when you two love-birds are re-joined. You can reward me then for my services as a go-between; a cup of wine will be enough.

PART IV

ACT III

Scene 1. The Western Chamber, the following morning

MOTHER: Red Maid, see if Little Nightingale is ready to go to the Pavilion of Farewell. The food is ready and Master Chang should have finished packing by now.

LITTLE NIGHTINGALE (aside): Today, alas, is the day. Goodbyes are sad at any time but how much more painful they are when the gray chill of autumn closes in. Dark clouds billow in the sky, casting their gloom over the flowers in the fields; the west wind blows strong and the wild geese are on the wing.

How sad to meet so late and part so soon! Would that I could delay his departure by tying these long willow branches to his horse, or by hindering the movement of the sun.

I have only just heard a gentle voice say, 'I love you' and now I hear it saying, 'I must go.' My bracelets grow loose and my body wastes away at the very sight of the Pavilion of Farewell.

Can anyone see the gloom in my heart? Is there anyone who understands my despair? The sight of the horse and carriage waiting to leave fill me with anguish. I do not want to play the charming young beauty; I want only to return to my bed where no

one can see the tears on my pillow. I am dying
with grief.

Scene 2. The Pavilion of Farewell

(Chang, who has been the first to arrive, walks forward
toward the carriages bringing Little Nightingale, her mother,
the Superior and Red Maid. As they get out, Little Nightingale
turns her face away.)

MOTHER: Ah, Master Chang. Now that you are one of
the family, it is no longer necessary for you and
my daughter to be apart.

(To Little Nightingale): Come, child.

Sit there, Master Chang. I will sit here and Little
Nightingale can sit there. Red Maid, pour some
wine.

(To Chang): Now that I have promised my daughter
to you, you must not disgrace her. You must make
every effort to come first in the Examination.

CHANG: With your blessing, a commission will be as
easy as picking up straw.

SUPERIOR (raising his cup of wine in a toast): The scholar
is not one who will be left behind.

LITTLE NIGHTINGALE (aside, sighing as they drink): The west
wind blows and the dead leaves scatter. The brown
misty grass is in mournful sway, and as I look at
him, withdrawn into his gloom, my eyes fill with
tears that I dare not let fall, lest the others know.
When they look, I lower my head and, with deep
sighs, pretend to arrange my white silk robe.

124

Others may see a happy future, but I see only a sad and tearful present so filled with the pain of love that I become weaker with each passing minute. After weeks of furtiveness and fear, we finally had a night in which our love was fully revealed and now we have to separate.

The heart-ache before we met was bad enough; who would have thought this could be ten times worse?

MOTHER: Red Maid, pour some more wine.

(Chang sighs.)

LITTLE NIGHTINGALE   (aside, looking at him): Are you thinking of your departure or your return? How do you look back on these past few weeks when your cheek rested on mine and we lay in each other's arms? Was it only a pleasant interlude?

Wouldn't it be better to stay together as happily as two lotus blossoms on a single stem? Why try for an official title? Isn't it ennobling enough to be the son-in-law of a Prime Minister?

This farewell dinner is ending too quickly — in another moment he will be gone. Were my mother not here, we could put propriety aside and sit close together like a happy couple. Instead, we are made to sit at separate tables while I try in vain to show my devotion to him with my eyes. And, as I look at him, I am suddenly petrified by an ancient vision — I see a faithful wife keeping a lonely vigil on a hilltop, waiting for her long-lost husband to return from sea as she is slowly turned to stone by the gods who take pity on her. Is that to be my

Farewell.

fate?

RED MAID: Mistress, you have eaten nothing yet. Have some soup.

LITTLE NIGHTINGALE: Oh, Red Maid, what kind of soup can I swallow? Everything I try to eat today is like clay and mud; in fact, it does not even have the aroma of clay or the flavour of mud. And the wine in my cup is as tasteless as water, filled as it is with my tears.

We are being torn apart for no good reason, he to one place and I to another with only our memories. The position he seeks is as unimportant to me as a snail's horn, the profit as small as a fly's head. As soon as this dinner ends, we will travel our separate ways, his horse heading east and my carriage west. Where will he be when the sun sets behind the green hills? Where will he sleep tonight? If I knew, it might be possible to find him in my dreams.

(Despite the presence of her mother and the Superior, she speaks openly to Chang): Come back quickly, whether you become a mandarin or not. It does not matter to me.

CHANG: I will come back at the top of the list.

LITTLE NIGHTINGALE: How sad that I have nothing to give you so you will remember me. Perhaps a verse . . .

> Deserted and cast off, what is to happen
> To me whose heart does burn?
> Will you give the love you so gently gave to
> The next one whose head you turn?

CHANG:

> In this world of ours there are many goodbyes
> And many a head that turns,
> But it is no simple thing to find another
> Whose heart forever burns.

LITTLE NIGHTINGALE: Our sleeves are wet with tears, yours perhaps as much as mine. As the nightingale flies east and the swallow heads west, I long to know the date of your return.

As you go, I would like to drink this cup of wine to you but, alas, I cannot. Before I can even bring it to my lips, my head reels, my eyes blur, and I grow faint.

I hope the weather favours you on your journey. Be moderate with food and drink and protect your health, so precious to me. Seek sleep early in the deserted villages along the way when it rains, and rise late at the country inns when the wind is cold. With no one to look after you in this autumn chill, give every attention to your well-being.

> Smiling, smiling together;
> We part crying, crying.

When I return home, I shall dread the sight of my bed where love dwelt so warmly last night under the embroidered coverlet. It will be cold tonight and you will be there only in my dreams.

I can think of nothing to detain you further, so mount your steed while both of us have courage in our tears.

I am not worried about your luck matching your learning at the Capital; whether you are first or not does not matter to me. I worry that you will give up this love for another.

Do not disappoint the wild geese who long to be your messengers and I will send frequent tidings with the golden carp.

If your name is not included in the list of honours, do not concern yourself. If you see fair beauties elsewhere, do not tarry as you have here.

CHANG: Sweet lady, who in this world could compare with you? It is only you I cherish.

(He turns his horse and rides off.)

LITTLE NIGHTINGALE (aside): My soul leaves me. If I could follow, even if only in my dreams . . .

The mist begins to come between us. The trees will soon hide him from view and, before long, the green hills will separate us completely.

How still it is with only the rustle of the grain in the wind; how long the road that leads into the setting sun!

RED MAID: Come, Mistress, your mother's carriage has already left.

LITTLE NIGHTINGALE: Let us return slowly to keep this night from ending too soon.

(They ride back silently.)

LITTLE NIGHTINGALE (along the way): Where do you think he is now? (A little later): He must be in the valleys between the hills, where the dying sun has already given up the day.

The sorrows of the world have gathered round me. How can this carriage carry such a burden?

(She weeps.)

PART IV

ACT IV

Scene 1. On the road to the Capital

CHANG (with his lute-boy): There is the Inn of the Grass Bridge, which means we have already made ten miles. This horse isn't going any farther tonight, so let's put up here and get an early start in the morning.

We are miles away from the Monastery and still I seem to see it behind the evening clouds. How vulnerable the lonely traveller is! On a slow horse, he becomes listless; in a strong wind, he is buffeted about like a broken line of wild geese. When he sees the leaves falling from the trees, his own separation makes him melancholy, and on the very first night it leaves a bitter taste.

Twenty-four hours ago, I lay under a coverlet filled with her fragrance, cheek to cheek. Her hair was like a cloud upon the pillow, her comb of jade emerging from it like a new moon. I loved her so intensely, I . . .

Ho! Innkeeper! Where are you!?

INNKEEPER: Here, Sir.

CHANG: Look after my horse and let me have your best room. I want nothing to eat, just a little sleep.

Scene 2. Inside the inn

(The innkeeper shows them to a room where there is only one bed.)

LUTE-BOY: I will spread my blanket on the floor at the foot of the bed. I am so tired.

(He is soon asleep.)

CHANG: What manner of sleep will come to me tonight? A lonely pillow in a lonely inn, the noise of insects all around and, to make matters worse, a strong sharp wind against the window pane. How long will it take to warm this thin coverlet?

(He tosses and turns, unable to sleep, and then hears the voice of Little Nightingale.)

VOICE: How long will it take through the lonely wilds and over the barren plains? Panting, out of breath, I must overtake him as quickly as I can.

I must go in, I must, despite my fear of the desolate darkness; my aching heart does not allow me to do otherwise.

When I saw you mount and ride off, I could no longer control my grief; I wept and began to waste away, unable to eat or sleep.

Our life together had only just begun when ambition took you away. From the heart-ache that preceded our meeting, we have been plunged into an even greater sorrow by our parting.

The long grass glistens and white frost covers the fallen leaves. The wind blows like fury along the rough and winding road but I must continue my search. Where are you? Where are you?

(There is the sound of knocking on the door.)

CHANG: Who is it? If you are a human being, reply. If you are a ghost, be gone!

VOICE: It is I. Open the door! Quickly!

CHANG (opening the door):   Come in, sweet Mistress. You must be frozen. Let me warm you.

LITTLE NIGHTINGALE: I cannot live without you. Take me with you.

CHANG: Where would I ever find another with a heart like yours, true against all odds. Look at your clothes, soiled and torn, your elegant shoes covered with mud. You must be exhausted. How were you able to come such a long way alone and on foot?

LITTLE NIGHTINGALE: I had to come, whatever the distance.

(She is too emotional to say any more and begins to cry.)

CHANG: Without sleep or food, your fragrant beauty has faded like a flower past its bloom. With your bed so lonely and cold, and the moon hidden behind the clouds, how could you not feel sad? Parting is the greatest burden we have to bear in life; I would rather we had not met than see you suffer so.

   I know now that it is neither a heroic nor powerful lover you wish, nor one who is proud and rich. Like me, you want only someone to share your pillow in life and, in death, the same grave.

SOLDIER (knocking on the door and calling out):   I just saw a young lady cross the river. She must have come into this inn. Light a torch and help me find her!

CHANG: Who is this? Stand behind me.

133

(He opens the door.)

LITTLE NIGHTINGALE (gasping as she sees the soldier): This is the bandit who attacked the Monastery and held his sword at my throat. This is the greatest rogue ever born, with the mind of a thief and the heart of a murderer.

SOLDIER: To what family does this young lady belong? How dare you hide her here?

LITTLE NIGHTINGALE: Be silent and withdraw or the 'White Horse General' will cut you to pieces for the vultures. Here he comes, riding his white charger!

(The soldier leaves quickly.)

CHANG (embracing Little Nightingale): My sweet love.

LUTE-BOY: Sir! What are you doing? Let go of me!

CHANG (waking up): Wha . . .! A dream! A nightmare in full gallop! Open the door, quickly!

The frost on the ground is unbroken and the morning mist is empty as the morning star rises and the moon fades in the early light. Where is my precious beauty?

LUTE-BOY: It is morning. Let us start out now and eat along the way.

CHANG: Ho! Innkeeper! My horse! And how much do I owe you?

Where are you, sweet Little Nightingale. Here we are a thousand hills and ten thousand streams apart. Why? For what?

PART V

ACT I

Scene 1. At the Capital six months later

CHANG: What news! What good news! It is unbelievable! The results of the Examination have been announced and I am at the top of the list — one of the three A's. I bow to you, my ancestors, for the good fortune you have brought.

I must get word to my sweet Little Nightingale at once to relieve her anxiety and let her know I shall be back.

But how soon? How long will it take to get my commission?

Ho, boy!

LUTE-BOY: Sir?

CHANG: Get me paper, brush, ink and stone; and prepare to leave for the Monastery at Hochung as soon as I get this letter finished. I want you to travel day and night to get it to Little Nightingale as soon as possible. When you see her, tell her I will follow as soon as I can. And don't forget to bring back a reply.

(Lute-Boy exits.)

(Aside): When last I saw her, the autumn leaves lay scattered across the withered fields. Today, the plum blossoms are already in bloom. With my nose in my books, autumn has changed to winter and winter to spring without my knowing.

135

Scene 2. At the Monastery, one month later

LITTLE NIGHTINGALE: All these months and still no news. I am beginning to fear the worst. What is to become of me? My face is colourless, my clothes are unkempt, and my hair ... look at it! How sorrowful and sad I have become!

My thoughts of him never cease. When I push my sorrow to the back of my mind, it inevitably returns. When I squeeze some of the grief from my heart, it appears on my brow which is scarcely large enough for all the frowns it has to bear.

The sorrow of today is piled on that of all the yesterdays in an unbearable burden and my tears flow into this mountain in a never-ending stream.

RED MAID: I have never seen you so pale and thin.

LITTLE NIGHTINGALE: I look out of my window to-ward the hills for some sign of happiness and see only barren trees and dead grass enveloped in a gray mist. In the river a boat lies motionless on the watery waste.

When I look into the mirror, my clothes do not seem to be mine. My skirt shows the creases of sleep and I have grown so thin that what was once an orderly row of buttons looks like a broken string of pearls. I shall soon be as thin as the stem of a chrysanthemum.

LUTE-BOY (Aside, arriving): They said I would find her here somewhere.

(He coughs to make his presence known.)

RED MAID: Who is it? Ah ... when did you arrive?

鶯鶯悶坐思憶張生

le Nightingale thinking about Scholar Chang.

Have you come by yourself or is your master with
you?

LUTE-BOY: My Master is still in the Capital. He has
sent me with this letter.

RED MAID: If it is not good news, you had better take
it back. My Mistress is in great distress . . . speak
up, boy, is it good news or not?

LUTE-BOY: I think so.

RED MAID (going over to where Little Nightingale lies half-
asleep on the couch): Good news, Mistress. Master
Chang has won an official post.

LITTLE NIGHTINGALE: This is no time for jokes.

137

RED MAID: His lute-boy is here with a letter.

LITTLE NIGHTINGALE: Give it to me and let me learn my fate. Now that the moment I have awaited has arrived, I dread it ... When did you leave the Capital? Where is your Master?

LUTE-BOY: I left about a month ago. When I set out, my Master was going about the streets having a merry time.

LITTLE NIGHTINGALE: That means he has won the highest honours. Do you not know that those at the top of the list must spend three days going about the streets to show themselves? Where is the letter?

LUTE-BOY (handing it to her): I think you are right, my lady.

LITTLE NIGHTINGALE (looking at the letter a moment before opening it): This is the first letter since his departure and only increases my sorrow by reminding me how long he has forgotten me ... I am staining the letter with my tears ... or are they the stains of his? Perhaps they are both, my sorrow covering his.

(She reads): 'Greetings, fair and sweet lady. Since we said farewell, half a year has suddenly passed and now, thanks to the protective blessings of my ancestors and your virtue, I have reached the top at the Examinations.

'I am unable to leave the Capital before obtaining my official appointment, so I am sending this letter to give you the good news and relieve any anxieties you might have.

'While I have been away, my heart has always

been with you. Do not be too harsh on me if I appeared to treat our love more lightly than the honour I sought at the Capital. You will know how great my love is when next we meet.

'Forget the melancholy of last night's lonely lantern and listen to today's happy twittering of the birds. I will soon be with you again.'

(Aside): He has hurdled the Examination as readily as my garden wall. His head was not turned by rouge or powder, nor was he lured away from the Examination Hall by the fatal temptations of the bedroom.

(To Lute-Boy):   Have you eaten yet?

LUTE-BOY: I have been waiting in your front hall since I arrived. When would I have eaten?

LITTLE NIGHTINGALE (to Red Maid): Get something for him.

LUTE-BOY: Would you write a reply for my master? He instructed me to return with it as soon as possible.

LITTLE NIGHTINGALE: Red Maid, a brush and some paper. Let me see ... I shall send him an inner garment of mine, a belt, a pair of stockings, a lute, a jade hairpin and a spotted bamboo brush.

Pack them carefully, Sister, and give the boy ten taels of silver for his journey back.

RED MAID: And what need has an official for such an odd collection?

LITTLE NIGHTINGALE: You do not know what is in my heart.

If he uses my inner garment as a nightgown, he and I will be together again. Wrapped inside it, he cannot help but feel my tenderness.

RED MAID: And the belt?

LITTLE NIGHTINGALE: The belt will enclose him in a circle of safety, protecting him on the right and left, from the front and behind.

RED MAID: And the stockings?

LITTLE NIGHTINGALE: They will keep him from wandering where he shouldn't.

RED MAID: He has a lute already. Why another?

LITTLE NIGHTINGALE: After he found me with his verse, the seven strings of the lute tied my heart to his. This lute is to remind him of our bonds.

RED MAID: What is the jade hairpin for?

LITTLE NIGHTINGALE: To remind him that I am not to be placed at the back of his head and forgotten, now that he has reached a position of honour.

RED MAID: And the spotted bamboo brush?

LITTLE NIGHTINGALE: The bamboos on the banks of the Hsiang were spotted with the tears an ancient Empress once shed when her Emperor died. The spots on this bamboo are to remind my love that the sleeves of my gown are also stained. The causes of grief are many but the sorrow that follows is always the same. One set of tears is no different from the next.

When you give the scholar these gifts, lad, tell him not to forget the love he left behind.

LUTE-BOY: I am ready to leave.

LITTLE NIGHTINGALE: Wait till the gifts are carefully packed and then take special care with them. Do not use the parcel as a pillow for that greasy head of yours. And be careful that it does not get soaked with rain.

My letter is near its end, but my love is only at its beginning. When I look out of the window for his return, all I see is the river coming toward me.

LUTE-BOY: I had better go.

LITTLE NIGHTINGALE: Tell your Master I am wasting away. He promised to return by the third day of the third moon, and the fourth moon has already come and gone. The trip to the Capital brought him rank but it has left me only with regrets.

PART V

ACT II

Scene 1. At the Capital one month later

CHANG: How ironic! I work myself to death to pass the Examination so I can marry Little Nightingale, and then get such a high grade I have to stay in the Capital for another two months because of this appointment to the Imperial College of Literature.

But I'm of no use to them here. How can I do anything when I'm too upset to eat or sleep? And it's no use their sending doctors around to see me. It is not a doctor I need.

The one they sent this morning guessed my trouble immediately. There are remedies for most diseases, he said, but not mine. There is no medicine for a lovesick heart.

What's keeping that boy so long? He should have been back by now. If anything has happened to Little Nightingale . . .

I would willingly die for you, sweet Little Nightingale, but all I do here is suffer. It has been half a year now and instead of feeling honoured and pleased by this appointment to a high post, I feel like a rootless wanderer in a strange country.

Hey, boy! Over here!

LUTE-BOY: When I got back, they told me you were unwell. Here is her letter.

CHANG: Why is the envelope stained? Are these tears of sadness or joy?

(He reads): 'How long have we been separated? Half a year? It seems more like three. I know now what they mean when they say that the Capital is farther than the sun.

'I was happy to learn from your letter that all has gone well with you. And, since it has, what more need I say? As your lute-boy is in a hurry to return, there is no time for me, in my present state, to better show my feelings than by sending you these few articles. They are insignificant and unworthy but I hope you will accept them for what they are, along with this verse:

"I looked longingly for the talented scholar,
Hoping he would not look longingly on another;
I heard of his high honours,
And looked in the mirror to see if I was worthy."

For this sweet lady I would gladly give up everything. Her brush has the power and strength of the finest calligraphers of our time; her literary talent is second to none.

How could I help but love her? Each article she sent has its special meaning:

The jade hairpin is herself — delicate and white, soft and smooth, lustrous and pure, without a flaw.

The belt is to encircle and protect our love.

The stockings are to keep my feet on the right path so that I always act with propriety.

The bamboo brush is the branch on which the male and female phoenix perch, spotted with tears like those of the ancient Empress who wept like my gentle maiden for her hero.

The lute is to keep my hands busy, my ears oblivious to distractions and my mind occupied.

Did my young lady say anything special?

LUTE-BOY: Only that she hopes you will avoid any other matrimonial entanglements, now that you have achieved a position of great promise.

CHANG: She still does not know my heart.

How forlorn this city, the monotony of the rain relieved only by gusts of wind. I sleep in fits and wake full of sorrow, unable to do anything but worry about how and when I shall return to the Monastery.

Sweet Nightingale ... having known you, how can I find my pleasure in darkened doorways. How could I be satisfied with a damaged flower or pluck a blossom that is not fresh?

How many beautiful and charming daughters of Prime Ministers do you think there are in the Capital whose families are looking for suitors? Even if there were one with your charm, where would I find one with your tender talents?

(To lute-boy): Take these things to my study. Empty one of the rattan boxes, spread some paper inside and put these items in carefully so that the sharp pricks of the rattan do not catch on the cotton and silk. If left in this bundle, they might become permanently creased; if exposed to the sun and wind, they might fade. Take every care when you pack them away.

(Boy exits.)

This love is what dreams are made of, but it is as solid as the earth. It will last until the seas run dry and the rocks wash away. This flame will burn until my candle and its tears are consumed. Like the silkworm, I will spin out my dreams until I die.

For six months there was nothing from her, not a jot of news or a line of verse. My longing for this letter nearly killed me, so sick was I in spirit. Everything is different now. This letter has taken possession of me.

PART V

ACT III

Scene 1. At an inn near the Monastery one month later

CHENG HENG (aside): What a predicament! We could have been wed by now! First her father dies. Then my father dies. Then this whole business with some starving scholar and suddenly I am without a bride.

This is going to take a bit of strategy. I can't just rush in and claim Little Nightingale.

RED MAID (Aside, arriving at the inn): What is going on? He is here and yet he does not come to see the Old Mistress. Instead, he asks to see me and my Mistress tells me to go ahead and find out what he wants.

(She knocks and Cheng Heng opens the door.)

Ten thousand greetings, Sir. My Mistress is wondering why you do not call on her.

CHENG HENG: I have only just arrived but will call as soon as I get settled. In the meantime, would you please ask my aunt if she would select an auspicious day for my wedding to Little Nightingale, now that the period of mourning is over? If you would help me in this matter, I will reward you well.

RED MAID: But Little Nightingale is already promised.

CHENG HENG: How can this be? How can a horse have two saddles? She was betrothed to me when her father was still alive. How can his widow go back on the word he has given?

RED MAID: Where were you when 'Flying Tiger' attacked with his army of bandit-soldiers? How would you marry her if they had carried her off?

Now that all the trouble is over, you come looking for her, but if it were not for Master Chang, she would not be here. Nor would the rest of us be alive today.

CHENG HENG: If she had been given to the son of a wealthy family, it would not have been so outrageous. But to be given to some half-starved wanderer is something else. How can he for a moment be compared with me, a man of high virtue from a noted family?

RED MAID: There have been no betrothal presents passed, nor have silks been sent to the bride's family. You have barely removed the dust of your journey and you want to marry the maiden at once, jumping under her silken coverlet without so much as taking off your shoes.

You and your high virtue!

You are not worthy of her. You would degrade someone as tender and beautiful as she.

When the Male and Female Essences were first separated into Heaven and Earth, the pure part became Heaven and the base part Earth, with Man between the two. Master Chang is a pure man, close to Heaven, but you Cheng Heng are of lowly clay.

CHENG HENG: How could he drive off an army of

bandits single-handedly? That is sheer nonsense.

RED MAID: When the Monastery was under siege and the Old Mistress promised Little Nightingale to anyone who could drive the brigands away, it was Master Chang who brought his friend, 'White Horse General', to the rescue. The Mistress had to act with sincerity and keep her promise.

CHENG HENG: How am I not this man's equal?

RED MAID: He is a hundred times better. How can you compare the full moon with a firefly? How can a learned gentleman be compared with an ignorant boor?

CHENG HENG: How can you compare him, a nobody, with me, the descendant of a long line of officials?

RED MAID: He, following the teachings of the sages, is devoted to the basic fundamentals of life. You use the position of your family to oppress people.

He, living on nothing and without grumbling, achieved high honours at the Capital by his own efforts. You got where you did on the backs of your forbears.

You think that officials should be selected from the families of officials and that the poor should remain poor. Your views are false, you wretched man! Look at the number of ministers and generals who have come from poor homes!

CHENG HENG: This whole affair must be the doing of that bald ass of a man who calls himself the Superior. I will thrash the matter out with him tomorrow.

RED MAID: You do not know a good man when you

see one. The old monk's thoughts are filled with charity and piety, and his days with good works. Your eyes are filled with unhappiness and your mouth is unrestrained with evil.

CHENG HENG: My betrothal to Little Nightingale was the dying wish of my uncle. I will come with sheep and wine tomorrow and we will set the date of the wedding.

RED MAID: You great bully! Do you think you can get by force what you cannot get any other way?

CHENG HENG: If my aunt turns me away, I shall get twenty or thirty of my friends to bring the young lady here and I will make her a married woman with or without your pious ceremonies.

RED MAID: So this is how the son of Minister Cheng gets what he wants – like a brutal brigand from the camp of 'Flying Tiger'. Nothing can save you from Hell, you abusive foul-mouthed bandit.

CHENG HENG: It's quite obvious whose side you're on, you little bitch. Get out! I will have Little Nightingale tomorrow. I am the one she will marry.

RED MAID: She will not marry you! She will not!

(She leaves.)

CHENG HENG (aside):   Something has been going on between that little bitch and Chang.

When I go to see my aunt tomorrow, I'll pretend I know nothing of what has happened and tell her, quite matter-of-factly, that I heard that Chang has already married the daughter of an official in the Capital. Being a great gossiper herself, she will believe what I tell her and come over to my side.

What else can she do with Little Nightingale then but give her to me?

You are a clever fellow, Cheng Heng, if I do say so myself. You cannot fail.

Scene 2. The Western Chamber the next day

MOTHER (aside): Now that my nephew is here to claim our daughter's hand, I should abide by the wishes of my husband. It would be improper for me to do otherwise.

CHENG HENG (entering and bowing): My dear aunt. Forgive me for entering unannounced but I saw no one outside.

MOTHER: My dear nephew, why did you not come earlier?

CHENG HENG: I did not have the face when I heard that Little Nightingale's betrothal to me had been broken.

MOTHER: The attempt by 'Flying Tiger' to kidnap Little Nightingale has caused us no end of trouble. The only way we could save ourselves from death was by promising her to whoever would save us. You were not here and we were quite helpless until Master Chang brought help.

CHENG HENG: Which Master Chang was that? One of the top three at the Imperial Examinations this year was named Chang.

MOTHER: That is the one. Chang Kung. Do you know him?

CHENG HENG: No, but I happened to see him when I was at the Capital. It was on the second day of the traditional three-day ride of the top three through the streets. When they were in front of the ornamental pavilions on the Imperial Road, the daughter of Minister Wei threw her embroidered ball at him and hit him. In fact, the ball almost hit me.

Ten of the servants of the family then pulled Chang off his horse and carried him to where the Minister was sitting. Chang shouted that he already had a wife but the Minister only laughed and said Imperial decree for this purpose; and that by tradition and law, he had to accept her as his number one wife. The wife he already had could be his number two wife, the Minister said.

MOTHER: How could the daughter of a Prime Minister be the second wife when the first is only the daughter of a Minister? I always said this Chang was not worthy of becoming a member of our family and he has now shown his true colours. Since he must marry Minister Wei's daughter, we shall have nothing more to do with him. I shall ask the Superior to select an auspicious day and hour for your wedding to Little Nightingale, my son.

(She leaves.)

CHENG HENG (aside): It worked! I must now get the gifts ready.

PART V

ACT IV

Scene 1. In the Monastery the next day

SUPERIOR (aside): I have just received word from the
Capital that Master Chang is on his way here to
take up his new post as Governor of this Prefecture.
I must arrange a welcoming ceremony for him at
the ten-mile Pavilion of Farewell.
(He exits.)

'WHITE HORSE GENERAL' (Aside, entering): What a happy
coincidence! First an Imperial decree placing me in
charge of military affairs in the Hochung Prefecture and then the news that my sworn brother
Chang Kung is to be the Governor. He is certain to
take advantage of this opportunity for an im-
mediate wedding to the beautiful Little Nightingale.
And who would be better suited to take charge of
the ceremonies than I? I had better call on the
Prime Minister's family to offer my good wishes.
(He exits.)

CHANG (aside): I never thought this moment would
arrive. I'm back, and with the Phoenix headdress
and red veil worn by the brides of officials. Where
are you, sweet Little Nightingale?
(Mother enters.)

  Mistress! As the new Governor of this Prefecture, I give you my greetings. As your son-in-
law-to-be, I pay my respects.

152

...olar Chang's return as a successful mandarin.

MOTHER: How can I accept your bows?

CHANG: Why do you look at me this way? Is something wrong? When I left for the Capital, you seemed very happy and gave me a special farewell dinner. Now that I have returned with a high position, your attitude is strangely different.

MOTHER: Don't pretend that you have been thinking of us. There is an old saying: 'Good beginning, good ending.' Without the one, how could I expect the other?

Although Little Nightingale is not particularly beautiful, she is, after all, the daughter of a Prime Minister. You would never have got close to her if

153

it were not for the brigands. And now that you have, you show a callous disregard for her by marrying the daughter of Minister Wei. Why have you done this?

CHANG: Who told you such a lie? If what you say is true, let the sky no longer give me cover, or the earth support. Let me fall victim to the vilest of afflictions and ills.

I do not deny that I saw beautiful maidens at the Capital; the streets are full of them. But my heart and mind were here, not looking for pleasures elsewhere.

Who is the rascal that has been stirring up trouble and dissension? Is it someone whose jealousy has produced a crafty tongue? If so, he should be strung from a pole in the market place.

MOTHER: It was Cheng Heng. It was he who told us how you became betrothed to the Minister's daughter when she hit you with her embroidered ball. If you don't believe me, ask Red Maid. (She calls): Red Maid!

RED MAID (entering and seeing Chang): So, you have come back to take your new office.

CHANG: Red Maid! How is your Young Mistress?

RED MAID: Since you have become the son-in-law of Minister Wei, we are now making the arrangements for her marriage to Cheng Heng, as originally planned.

CHANG: How can anything be more grotesque? How can Little Nightingale take a greasy monkey like him for a husband? How can you serve such a black cat?

RED MAID: Spare us your anger. Have you been happy since we saw you last? Where do you keep your new bride and how does she compare with my Young Mistress?

CHANG: I did not expect you to be taken in by this nonsense. The others may not know how I suffered because of my love for Little Nightingale but you know only too well.

This was to be a happy day. Why is it turning into such a miserable one? If I have a bride anywhere else but here, let me be struck dead on this spot.

I have gone through a lonely hell and worked myself to death to win the title of 'Lady' for my love. I brought it back with an overwhelming feeling of joy and delight and now that I am ready to give it to her, I find that you have dug my grave.

RED MAID (to Mother): I told you he was not the kind of person you thought him to be. I shall tell my Young Mistress he is here.

(She goes into the bedroom and returns with Little Nightingale.)

CHANG: My sweet sweet lady.

LITTLE NIGHTINGALE: A thousand blessings on you, Sir.

RED MAID: Have you nothing else to say?

LITTLE NIGHTINGALE: What is there to say? I had prepared no end of things but, now that he is here, everything has changed and I am left with nothing but deep sighs. I long to unfold the sorrows of my heart but I cannot even look at him. All I can do is wish him every blessing and ask why he has abandoned me for the daughter of Minister Wei.

CHANG: Who told you I have done so?

LITTLE NIGHTINGALE: Cheng Heng told my mother.

CHANG: Why does everyone listen to this villain? Is it only Heaven that knows what is in my heart? Ever since I left, I have given no other maid a second glance and now, for no good reason, I am being accused of marrying a girl whose shadow I have not even seen. If I have, may my family perish and our line come to an end.

(To Red Maid): Did you and your Mistress invite Cheng Heng to come?

RED MAID: I did all I could to help you and now you are abusing me. This family has always been upright and pure, its forbears worthy and good. Why would any of its members invite a foul-tongued villain, who cannot tell white from black, to soil this beauty with his ugliness? My Young Mistress would never lower herself enough to consider marriage to such a worthless fish.

To her, you are the God of Spring, her lord and master. Why would this tender flower invite the axe of a common wood-cutter? I am bursting with fury at this monster's destructive plotting.

MOTHER: Call Cheng Heng and let each man tell his story. Then we will decide who to believe.

LITTLE NIGHTINGALE: Let us ask the 'White Horse General' to settle this matter. The man who saved us from the bandits can help us punish the one who is trying to cheat the other of his bride.

MOTHER: Red Maid, take your Young Mistress to her room.

(Red Maid and Little Nightingale exit.)

'WHITE HORSE GENERAL' (entering):   Well,   my   brother, we meet again at last. I heard the good news and came to wish you well.

CHANG: I returned expecting to find a happy bride but find, instead, that everything is in a state of turmoil because of some scurrilous report about my being married in the Capital. And now she wants to give Little Nightingale to the one who spread this foul rumour.

CHENG HENG (entering):   I am here with my gifts, ready for the wedding.

CHANG: So this is Cheng Heng. Why are you here, villain?

CHENG HENG: You must be ... ah ... ah ... yes, Master Chang. I heard you were first in the Examinations so I came to offer my congratulations.

'WHITE HORSE GENERAL':   How dare you try to steal the bride of an honest man?

CHANG: I plan to report this to the Throne and have you executed.

'WHITE HORSE GENERAL':   Take the advice of the cuckoo in that green willow out there. It is saying, 'Go home, go home.' If you don't clear out, I shall arrest you here and now.

CHENG HENG: There is no need for that. Let Master Chang proceed with his wedding.

MOTHER: Don't do anything rash, General. It will be enough to turn him out.

CHENG HENG: I am finished. How can I return to my

people after this loss of face? Now that my scheme has failed, there is only one thing left to do . . . if I can find the courage to do it.

(He leaves.)

MOTHER: I hope he doesn't blame me. I am, after all, his aunt.

'WHITE HORSE GENERAL': Let us begin the celebration and see to it that this young couple are happily united.

IMPERIAL MESSENGER (entering with proclamation): Peace reigns throughout the world and the mountains echo the cries of 'Long Live the Emperor' from his loyal subjects and the officials of the surrounding states who come to pay their respects.

Benevolent in peace and righteous in battle, His Majesty excels in good deeds and his Court is worthy and good.

Under the rule of Heaven, the people are prosperous and the ten-thousand-mile river flows through the land untroubled. The harvests are bountiful and the people live in peace throughout this happy land which will once more see the arrival of the phoenix and the unicorn.

The sacred and wise Emperor of the T'ang Dynasty has issued a decree sanctioning this marriage and hopes that lovers throughout the world, like these two, will live together happily to the end of their lives and throughout eternity.